FABLES
FOR THE
NUCLEAR
AGE

FABLES
FOR THE
NUCLEAR
AGE

ALAN NEIDLE

Illustrations by Jeff Leedy

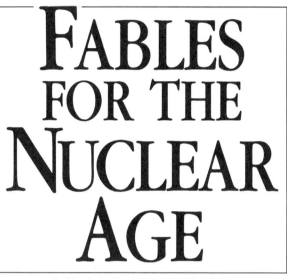

PARAGON HOUSE
New York

First edition, 1989

Published in the United States by

Paragon House Publishers
90 Fifth Avenue
New York, NY 10011

Text design by Robin Malkin

Library of Congress Cataloging-in-Publication Data
Neidle, Alan F.
Fables for the nuclear age
/Alan Neidle.—1st ed.
p. cm.
ISBN 1-55778-073-0   **3** 1 MAY **'**89
1-55778-182-6 (pbk.)
1. Fables, American. I. Title.
PS3564.E294F3   1988
818'.5402—dc19   88-3776
                                          CIP

Manufactured in the United States of America

To my wife, Diana, whose intelligence, patience, and sense of humor were vital. In fact, she thought of some of the funniest ideas in this book—and persuaded me to abandon some of the worst.

To my daughters, Louise and Betsy, who will, I hope, see a time when those in charge dig fewer ditches for us to jump into.

And to the animals, the four-legged ones, who go on doing what has to be done, with shrewdness, steadiness, and lack of self-consciousness. They know who they are. Of course, they would never indulge in the follies which I have unfairly attributed to many of them. I hope they will forgive me.

CONTENTS

Thinking Big—
Thinking Wrong—
And Thinking
Not At All

The Pikes Who Hated Each Other

THERE WERE ONCE two pikes who inhabited a small lake. These ferocious fish hated each other with a total, all-consuming passion.

"This lake is not big enough for the two of us," said one of the pikes to the other. "Prepare to meet your maker!"

"Say your prayers!" demanded the other pike. "You are about to depart this vale of tears."

With that, the two pikes swam at each other with lightning speed. As they approached the point of collision, both pikes opened their mouths as wide as they could.

One pike happened to spread his jaws just a little wider than the other. Suddenly one of the pikes found his head and half of his body wedged tightly into the body of the other.

And that is the way they remained until their deaths—inseparably joined together in their hatred.

The Jaguar Who Possessed The Most Advanced Weapon In The World

IN THE JUNGLES of South America there once lived a jaguar who was viewed by all the other animals as a scourge. This big cat had a deadly technique for dispatching every type of creature. When a column of wild pigs dashed through the jungle, the jaguar would drop down from a branch onto the back of any straggler. To catch fish in the river, he patted his tail on the water in imitation of falling fruit. If he found a giant turtle, he would flip him over with his paw, bite a hole between his back and front shields, and scoop out the flesh. Even the alligators weren't safe since the jaguar was adept at breaking their necks and then tearing their armor off.

The jaguar often used a particularly fearsome tactic against howler monkeys. The howlers would tremble in the highest branches. From the base of the tree the jaguar would gaze upward, fixing on one of the monkeys the steadiest, most malevolent stare ever achieved by any animal. The monkey, knowing what would be in store for him if he slipped, would get increasingly fidgety and begin to hop nervously from branch to branch. When the tension became unbearable the howler monkey would, in the end, lose his balance and plop down at the feet of the jaguar. Monkey meat, which the jaguar was especially partial to, was his simply for the staring.

Now the animals of the jungle were so distressed by the ravages inflicted by this jaguar that they convened a meeting of potential victims to see what could be done. Not surprisingly they were long on wringing their paws and short on solutions. But finally a spider monkey who was noted for his shrewdness announced that he could solve the problem—although he refused to divulge his

5

plan. The other animals, seeing no alternative, agreed to let the spider monkey have a go at bringing down the jaguar.

A few days later, choosing his timing with great care, the spider monkey approached the jaguar when he was stuffed with pig and rather content with the world. "Renowned jaguar," began the spider monkey in a tone of reverence, "your prowess as a mighty hunter fills all of us with awe—that is, all of us who are able to maintain our objectivity."

The jaguar was suspicious of flattery although, like all great creatures, he was not entirely immune to it. "Why are you presuming to break in on my rest?" he asked.

"Well, you see," answered the monkey, "I would be privileged to offer you a suggestion which if you thought it had merit might increase your power even beyond its present legendary dimensions."

"All right, let's hear it," commanded the jaguar.

"I could not help noticing," continued the monkey, "that you possess a most unusual secret weapon, but I must confess to being a little puzzled that you do not make much greater use of it."

"And what do you consider to be my secret weapon?"

"Truly it is nothing short of marvelous that you can stare up in the trees at howler monkeys and then they will drop down at your feet ready to be eaten."

"Yes, that is a special talent of mine," conceded the jaguar. "But why do you call it a secret weapon?"

"Just think of what you are accomplishing," answered the monkey. "It must be that you are directing invisible beams from your eyes straight to the howler monkey and that these mysterious beams are so powerful that they make the howler take leave of his senses."

"Well, I hadn't quite thought of it that way. But your description does seem apt."

"Do you realize, mighty jaguar, that no other animal possesses this amazing weapon? Not even those creatures who call themselves human beings."

"And what is your suggestion to increase my power?" asked the jaguar who, in spite of himself, was growing more and more intrigued.

"Now if I were lucky enough to be in your skin," said the spider monkey, "and I possessed your amazing weapon, I would use it all the time. Then there would be no need for exhausting struggles with tapirs. I wouldn't have to waste my strength tearing apart alligators. All I'd have to do is calmly fire off beams from my eyes and, plop, I'd have all the food I wanted."

"Yes, I begin to see your point," said the jaguar.

"And what's more," added the spider monkey, "your fame would spread far and wide. You would be held in awe everywhere as the jaguar who knew how to use the most advanced weapon in the world."

"Thank you. Thank you," said the jaguar.

"It has been a pleasure to serve such a great animal," said the monkey, who then took his leave.

The weeks and months that followed were a little hard on the howler monkeys. They became the principal staple in the jaguar diet. Never having learned of the spider monkey's plan it was understandable that they began to feel that there had been no plan in the first place. In fact, they came near to abandoning all hope for deliverance.

The jaguar, on the other hand, was entirely pleased with the situation. He spent most of the time resting at the base of trees underneath frightened howler monkeys. Every now and then he lifted his head upwards, fired off his beam weapon, and ate.

Now in time some changes began to take place in the physique of the jaguar. Never having to chase after tapirs his calf muscles became flabby. Never having to hang on to squirming pigs his biceps became feeble. Never having to tear open crocodiles his nails became tender. Naturally the jaguar was not conscious of this deterioration. He was reveling in the self-satisfaction of possessing the most wonderful weapon in the world.

From a distance the spider monkey watched and waited patiently. When he judged that enough time had passed, he organized a gang of the roughest and most vindictive animals in the jungle to attack the jaguar.

What happened next is decidedly not pretty to relate. After a furious scuffle, the enfeebled and panting jaguar was gored in the stomach by the tusks of a boar. A boa constrictor threw his coils around the jaguar and held him tight while a turtle slapped him in the face with his flippers. Several giant rodents added to his torment. At one point the jaguar tried to use his secret weapon. But these tough characters were impervious to the beams from the jaquar's eyes. In the end the coup de grace was delivered by the jaws of a crocodile.

Now the main action of this story is over. But a word should be added about the reaction of the howler monkeys when they learned of the special role they had unwittingly played in the spider monkey's plan. They were incensed and they chased the spider monkey all over the jungle. However, their indignation did not last long. With the passage of time and after some reflection they came to accept that their sacrifice had been essential. Indeed they even took considerable pride in it, recounting their role to other jungle animals in ever more heroic terms.

The Animals Of The Jungle
Who Held A Symposium
About The Nature Of War

IN THE SHRINKING RAIN forest of Borneo the great animals of the jungle were thrown together more and more frequently. On one occasion they found themselves engaged in a most unusual activity. In the crown of a tall tree they were conducting a symposium on one of the world's supreme issues—the nature of war.

The panther took the position that war was absolutely natural and that it provided an excellent opportunity for all creatures to prove their worth. A gibbon, while conceding that everyone would probably have to live with it, declared that war was a horror and

a waste, and that it was even out-of-date. The python believed that the muscle tone of all animals who lived in the jungle would deteriorate if war were abolished, but he wasn't too worried that this would happen since it was inevitable, as he put it, for some to be crushed and others to do the crushing. An orangutan, taking a somewhat more cerebral view, stated that war was a superb subject for research and analysis so that its manifestations, dynamics, and consequences could be comprehended by all animals.

Now these exchanges were rather taxing intellectually. In fact, they were so demanding that they required the absolute attention of the participants. And so the animals did not hear a buzzing sound which at first was faint but then grew louder all around them until finally the human beings on the ground below took their chain saws and cut through the base of the very tree in which the animals were conducting their symposium. It was one of the last trees in the jungle and it crashed to the ground—ending, among other things, the animals' fascinating debate on the nature of war.

The Boobies Who Tried
To Cap The Volcano

ONCE UPON a time on a volcanic island in the Pacific Ocean there lived a colony of bluefooted boobies. These large gooselike birds, who possessed long strong bills, piercing yellow eyes and big bright blue webbed feet, made their nests on the floor of the volcano's crater. It was an enormous area, flat and round, covered by small stones and a few scraggly bushes. The rim of the crater loomed high above.

The leader of the colony was an old bird who wanted very badly to go down in booby history as a great statesman. And so, one day, he convened his cabinet—consisting of the Minister of Foreign Affairs, the Minster of Defense and the Minister of Engineering—to announce a new program. They met on a ledge near the rim of the crater.

"Look down below you," said the leader. "There on the floor of the crater are thousands of fellow boobies. I am determined to bring about a safer future for all of them." The ministers all gazed down at the throng of boobies far below. Some were sitting on nests. Some were parading around to attract mates. And some were circling in the air. They were going over the rim to the ocean or coming back with fish for their young ones. The ministers could also see that many of the birds on the ground were fluttering their wings to create a little breeze. Others were rocking on their heels to keep their feet from getting too hot.

The leader resumed his presentation. "It's been a long time since this volcano has erupted. But I'm old enough to remember the last eruption. It was a terrible event. Red-hot mud poured out of the mountain. Thousands of boobies and their chicks were killed. We must find a way to prevent that from ever happening again. In fact, I have conceived a plan for capping the volcano."

11

The booby ministers were used to hearing grandiose schemes from their leader. It would be best to listen to him patiently. "What is your plan?" asked the Booby Foreign Minister politely.

"I believe," said the leader, "that the next eruption will come from those cracks down there." They all looked way down at a corner of the floor of the crater where there were several long black fissures in the earth. Fumes were rising out of them. "Our task will be to stuff those cracks solid. We will ask all the boobies to collect twigs and leaves and stones—all the things we use for nests—and to fly down and drop them in the cracks. Then the mixture can be sealed with fish meal which the boobies can insert with their bills. What do you think?" The leader was addressing the Minister of Engineering.

"Well," answered the minister, "it is a wonderful conception, but I have a few questions about its implementation." The Minister of Engineering also remembered the last eruption. But he could not imagine how a few twigs stuffed in a crack would block a volcano. Knowing from long experience that it would not be politic to question the leader's vision, he said, "I wonder, will the fish meal be a strong enough glue?"

"You may have a point there," the leader answered. "Perhaps we should use booby droppings. We can make plenty of that. I will look to you to conduct tests as to which is the more reliable cement."

"There are some other problems," said the minister, who did not wish to give up so easily. "Our boobies use twigs and leaves for nests. Will they be willing to give these up for filling cracks in the earth? If we do need to use fish meal, will they agree to sacrifice so much of their catch? Their chicks will be hungry. But I'm most worried about what it will be like for the boobies flying just over those cracks. A lot of them are going to get sick from the fumes and the heat down there."

The booby leader responded with vehemence. "No great task is ever easy. What's a little discomfort when the future of the booby race is at stake?" The leader sensed that his cabinet could use some inspiration. He therefore stretched his neck, raised his bill toward the sky, and began parading around. One after the other, he lifted his blue webbed feet high into the air. This performance usually produced awe in other boobies since the leader had the largest and most brilliantly colored feet.

"I am the supreme booby," continued the leader. "I am not just a politician who does what's cheap and easy. I am a statesman. Thousands of boobies are counting on me. I will inspire them to great effort, as I have just inspired you. When our task has been accomplished, all the boobies will be grateful. So will all the creatures who live in the crater with us—the little finches, the tortoises, the lizards, and even the snakes."

Immediately after the meeting, the leader descended to the crater floor and delivered a stirring oration to thousands of boobies. Soon, boobies were flying around with twigs and leaves in their bills and were dropping them into the steaming fissures. The Minister of Engineering, in accord with his responsibility to supervise the effort, was issuing a series of shrill whistles. These provided air control so that the boobies would not collide head-on as they dived toward the cracks.

But the minister was far from happy in his work. As he had feared, some boobies were getting dizzy from the heat and the fumes. Some became so sick that they were forced to drop out. All the while, to inspire his followers, the booby leader paraded back and forth on a ledge just above the scene of activity. In the brilliant sunlight, his huge webbed feet shone an intense blue as he lifted them with great pomp and solemnity, one after the other.

That night, after work had ceased, the Minister of Engineering sought out his old friend, the Minister of Foreign Affairs. "I am deeply disturbed," he said. "We all know what a foolish project this is. It will ruin the health of lots of boobies—and nothing will be accomplished. Should we not protest to the leader, and if he doesn't listen to reason, shouldn't we offer to resign?"

"That would be disloyal to the leader," snapped back the Foreign Minister.

"But we have loyalties to the booby colony also—not just to the leader."

"You have a peculiar notion of loyalty," said the Foreign Minister. "The leader needs our support most when he is engaged in a dubious venture. Anyone can be loyal when they agree completely with a policy. That's easy. What's really needed is loyalty when you disagree and you know something is stupid."

When the Minister of Engineering got home to his nest near the rim of the crater, his spouse was awaiting him anxiously. As was their custom, they stroked each other affectionately on both sides of their long bills. The minister's supper was ready—a pile of fish which had been supplied by other boobies. That was one of the many perks, like the assignment of cool nesting sites on the crater's rim, which the leader insisted be provided for the ruling circle. The minister told his spouse about the day's events. They reached rapid agreement that the next day he would make frank and firm representations to the leader about why the new project should be halted.

When the Minister of Engineering had his private meeting with the leader, he set forth fully all his objections. The leader answered with friendliness, "I value highly your readiness to speak frankly with me. It is only natural, however, that you and I should see things differently. Yours is the perspective of the engineer. You are too wrapped up in the details. I, on the other hand, have the broad vision of the statesman. I am an optimist. I cannot give up on a project which promises such great benefits for future booby generations. I know I can count on your full and continuing support. Do not forget—you will need to start tests soon on whether fish meal or bird droppings will provide the better cement."

That day the work continued as before. But there was little visible progress. The twigs and leaves either missed the fissures entirely or dropped down them without a trace. More and more birds showed signs of exhaustion. A few circled up toward the edge of the crater but failed to make it over the top. They crashed into the rim, fell between boulders and, unable to escape, perished.

In the evening the Minister of Engineering approached the Minister of Defense. He again laid out his objections to the project and asked whether resignation was not the best course to follow. The Booby Minister of Defense was shocked. "Have you taken leave of your senses?" he asked. "What do you think you will accomplish by resigning? You will just be relieved of your position and then you will have none of your perks. You will have to live like all the other boobies—no piles of fish supplied every night, no cool nesting place on the best part of the crater. Is that what you want?" He paused, fixed his companion with an intense stare from his yellow eyes and declared finally, "My friend, what do you think this is—some kind of fairy tale? You'll make a grand gesture and then there'll be no more foolishness in the world?"

The Minister of Engineering was deeply discouraged when he returned home to his spouse. After their mutual bill stroking, the minister reviewed the opinions of his friends, the Foreign Minister and the Defense Minister. She, however, was not impressed. "Do you know what those two are doing now?" she asked. "They're making speeches all over the booby colony proclaiming that only a genius could have conceived the idea of capping the volcano."

The minister's spouse insisted that they must make a joint decision about his resignation. "We have spent many years together," she said. "We have always taken turns sitting on the nest and bringing back food for our young. Let us now face together the greatest challenge of your life." They spent a long time weighing all the different arguments. In the end they decided that the minister would make one final appeal to the leader in the morning and then he would resign if his advice was again rejected. "And you should be prepared to announce your reasons not just to the leader but before the whole company of boobies," added the minister's spouse. "Since we have agreed this is a joint decision, I will stand by your side."

At daybreak the Minister of Engineering and his spouse flew to the ledge on which the leader, who had already arrived, conducted his inspirational parades. Work was about to resume to stuff the fissures on the crater's floor. The minister called aside the leader and again reviewed his objections to the project. He declared that if the work continued he would feel compelled to resign and would explain to all the boobies why he could not be associated with a project which would only harm booby society.

The leader accused the minister of disloyalty. When the minister did not back down, the leader began to hiss at him. Then he thrust his long bill at him and flapped his wings in an intimidating fashion. At this point the minister's spouse asserted herself. She moved in front of the leader and flapped her wings violently at him. Since she was a much larger bird, as all booby females are, the leader quickly realized that his bullying tactics would not work.

"You know," said the leader, "I have pledged to save future generations of boobies from the terror of the volcano. My plan may not necessarily be the best. If you can think of a better one, I will consider it."

The Minister of Engineering thought hard for a few moments. Then he and the leader huddled together. The leader immediately decided to address the throng of boobies who were about to start the morning's labor to cap the volcano.

"My friends," he began, "I have been dissatisfied by progress in capping the volcano. I know you have all worked hard. But I am deeply concerned about the harmful impact on booby health from the volcano's fumes. I therefore directed our distinguished Minister of Engineering to provide me with an analysis of all aspects of the problem. Based on his study, I have devised a simple solution to all our difficulties. When the present egg laying season is over and our new chicks are strong enough to fly over the rim of the crater, let us all leave this place. I will lead you to a beautiful beach on a nearby island. We will never again have to worry about destruction from the volcano." The boobies whistled in appreciation.

"Our nests," continued the leader, "will be right next to the best fishing in the world." There was a crescendo of whistling.

"Young boobies will never again crash into the rim of the volcano." All the boobies were grunting and whistling with happiness.

"And most important of all," shouted the leader, "when you parade around the nest you will no longer burn your beautiful blue feet on hot stones." A pandemonium of booby shrieks filled the crater.

The spouse of the Minister of Engineering was more than a little put out that her mate had received so little credit. But the minister was satisfied. He knew what really mattered.

PROVIDING
FOR THE
NATIONAL
INSECURITY

The Crocodile Who Demanded Absolute Security

A VAST CROWD of crocodiles made their home along the shore of a river in Africa. Their leader, who was two hundred years old, was of gigantic size—more than twice the length and girth of any other crocodile. He bore many scars from past battles. A chunk of tail and part of one claw had been torn away in some ancient encounter.

The crocodiles, about two thousand strong, dominated their stretch of the river. Nevertheless, they suffered occasional casualties at the hands of others. Just recently a huge hippo had crushed a few medium-size crocodiles in his great jaws. And baboons, mongooses and vultures sometimes gobbled up baby crocs and crocodile eggs.

The old crocodile chief did not like this at all. He felt that the crocodiles should be free from harassment by other animals. So

he assembled the crocodile council, composed of the roughest and shrewdest crocodile veterans.

"Our security is terrible," croaked the crocodile chief. "Fat hippos savage some of our clan. And infant crocs are being killed by all kinds of animals."

"Well, so what?" said one old warrior. "We dish out a lot more punishment than we take." These crocodiles on the council had pretty thick skins.

"I believe," said the chief, "that we should be satisfied with nothing less than absolute security. We deserve it. We have the numbers and the strength. By the way, did I ever tell you the story about the time I chewed up a giraffe?" The chief fixed his comrades with a steely gaze. "I took one big bite and cut through the giraffe's thigh-bone like it was a monkey's arm."

A council member returned to the main issue. "Absolute security—that's a pretty tall order. I assume we're going to keep on eating others?" The chief nodded in agreement. "How," continued the council member, "are the other animals going to take it when we say they can't ever eat us but we keep on eating them?"

"Are you getting soft?" responded the chief. "What happens to other animals is their problem, not ours. We should be interested in just one thing—our own security. You remember that time an antelope got in the way when I was about to eat a python? I took the antelope in my jaws and with one snap of my head tossed him across the river. You can be sure that antelope learned to keep his mind on his own security."

The other crocodiles had heard their venerable leader tell these anecdotes many times. After a respectful pause another council member resumed the discussion. "There's one more problem, chief. All of us like to eat baby crocodiles. You, yourself, must have eaten thousands over the years. How are we going to tell others that they can't eat baby crocs but we can?"

"I'm surprised you don't know the answer yourself," said the crocodile chief. "When we eat baby crocs that's strictly an internal affair. It's nobody else's business.

The crocodiles on the council knew that their chief was very strong-willed. They had raised the essential questions. But it was obvious that "absolute security" was to be the order of the day. The chief broke the silence: "I'm glad all of you see it my way.

You know I didn't get to be two hundred years old by being sentimental about security."

The council then adopted a plan of action to achieve absolute security. Crocodile defenses would be greatly strengthened. Patrols by the fiercest crocodiles would kill all animals found in peripheral areas which bordered on crocodile territory. Within their territory, everyone would be cleared out or killed except those animals whose absolute loyalty could be counted upon, like the little birds who cleaned the teeth of the crocodiles.

When the crocodiles began to implement their new policies, a great hue and cry arose among the other animals—at least among those who remained alive to make a hue and cry. Who did these crocodiles think they were to demand absolute security for themselves even while they continued to attack others? Didn't they realize that absolute security for the crocodiles meant absolute insecurity for everyone else? Things were already tough enough in the jungle without the crocodiles pursuing outlandish notions.

But the rest of the animals were at a loss as to what they could do. How could a handful of smaller animals like baboons, mongooses and storks—even if they were reinforced by a few dozen hippos—ever hope to take on several thousand determined crocodiles?

So the animals decided to seek help. They approached a nearby herd of elephants. The leader of the elephants sympathized with the outrage of the other animals. The old bull had seen a great deal of life and knew that no one, not even the mightiest, could ever be completely safe. Only recently his beloved mate had suffered a gruesome demise after a huge and exceptionally venomous black mamba had bitten her between the toes. Why should the crocodiles think they were entitled to absolute security?

The elephant leader agreed to help the other animals. He organized a platoon of the fiercest bull elephants. They stampeded into the territory of the crocodiles and when they found the lair of the crocodile chief and some of his closest associates they trampled all over them.

The leader of the elephants lifted the flattened crocodile chief in his trunk and flung him into the crotch of a tree where everyone could see him. "That's for absolute security," bellowed the bull elephant leader.

The Frog Who Protested
Against Aggression

ONE DAY deep in the woods a confrontation occurred between two snakes and an equal number of frogs. The snakes stared intently at the frogs. Entranced, the frogs gazed back.

Suddenly there was a blur of movement and one of the frogs found his head and torso inside the snake's mouth and his feet kicking in the air.

The second frog was jolted into speech, "I must protest. We have done you no harm. Your associate has committed naked aggression."

"Nonsense," replied the snake whose mouth was not full of frog. "I saw clearly what happened. That frog leaped viciously at my friend's face. Undoubtedly he intended to choke him." The protesting frog was at a loss for words.

"Indeed," continued the snake, "it is clear from the bellicose manner in which you press these unfounded accusations that you, too, are planning aggression."

Once more there was a blur of movement and the second frog also found himself in the mouth of a snake.

The Water Buffalo Who Was Warned

In Asia a herd of wild water buffaloes, being possessed of huge bulk and black faces, had intimidated all the other animals. These buffaloes were utterly confident about their place in the world. Indeed, it had been a long time since anything had disturbed their well-settled routine—lots of leisurely grazing on succulent plants, lovemaking whenever the spirit moved them, and endless mud baths.

One day the buffaloes were visited by some mynah birds who made it their business to spread stories, especially about unusual events. "We have incredible news," said one of the birds. "There's a swarm of moths up in the jungle and they're sucking blood from all the big animals—pigs, tapirs, and even a tiger."

"That's preposterous," said the biggest buffalo, who happened to be the leader of the herd. "Such things just don't happen. I've been around a good many years and I've never seen a vampire moth."

"Well, we've seen them," answered the mynah birds.

"And will you please tell me," asked the leader of the water buffaloes with considerable scorn, "just how moths suck blood?"

"We got up close," answered a mynah bird. "We saw little tubes come out from their heads and then they stuck them into the necks of the animals while they were sleeping."

"You must be having hallucinations," said the buffalo leader. "You've been eating too many ripe berries." The water buffaloes settled back into their comfortable routine and the mynah birds flew off.

A few days later the mynah birds returned. "Those moths! They are really something! Last night they sucked blood from some oxen. And this morning those poor beasts were in such terrible shape that they couldn't even get up on their feet."

The leader of the water buffaloes was irritated. "Why are you spreading these wild fantasies? Don't you have something better to do?"

"In fact," declared one of the birds, "the moths happen to be heading this way. You would be well advised to stop lolling about in the mud and to begin planning defensive measures."

"This is quite ridiculous," snorted the leader of the water buffaloes. "I'm not going to change our way of life just because of some crazy rumors." Once again the mynah birds flew away.

Next day several pigs stumbled into the field where the buffaloes were grazing. They had just fled from the jungle. The pigs were covered with red sores. Some of them could scarcely stand. They did not seem to know what had happened to them.

The mynah birds swooped down and started jabbering at the water buffaloes. "You see! You see! We told you so!"

"This proves absolutely nothing," said the leader of the water buffaloes with great vehemence. He was angry because he had been forced to rise from his morning mud bath. "This can't be the work of vampire moths because there aren't any vampire moths. These dumb pigs probably stuck their heads in some poison plants."

A few water buffaloes nevertheless were frightened. They urged that they should all seek shelter in nearby caves during the night and that the leader should institute a system of guard duty.

The leader was getting angrier and angrier. "What do you think we are? Gerbils? Salamanders? Are we supposed to cower in fear of a few moths? Water buffaloes, I would remind you, are mighty animals. We must act in accord with our stature."

Impressed by the confidence of their leader and intimidated by his vehemence, the water buffaloes resumed their familiar ways. The remainder of the day was filled with grazing, mud bathing and amorous encounters. When the sun set the buffaloes found themselves pleasantly spent and fully satisfied with their existence. They plopped down on the ground for a good sleep.

As the sun rose next morning, the water buffaloes began to stir. A few tried to get to their feet but stumbled and collapsed. There were red sores all over their heads and necks. Many, despite their feebleness, felt an irresistable compulsion to roll on the ground to assuage an intense itchiness.

The leader of the water buffaloes finally made it to his feet. In halting, barely audible tones he spoke to his herd. "The moths—they couldn't have done this by themselves. We've been betrayed. Those mynah birds," the leader gasped for breath, "they must have led the moths right to us. We've been done in—by traitors."

The leader collapsed to the ground. From the field of water buffaloes nothing could be heard but the sound of groaning.

The Sharks Who Engaged
In Espionage

ONCE UPON A TIME in the tropical waters of the Atlantic Ocean a school of hundreds of hammerhead sharks entered into an alliance with a large herd of loggerhead turtles. The sharks considered that they had achieved a great coup of statesmanship. The alliance, of course, could hardly be considered essential from a strictly strategic standpoint. Hundreds of determined hammerhead sharks were a pretty formidable force—with or without allies.

What the sharks most valued was the diplomatic impact of the alliance. The hammerheads were not given to self-delusion. They knew they were hated throughout the ocean. They understood that their unusual visage—a flat T-shaped head with eyes popping out the sides and a gaping mouth bristling with teeth—inspired terror in others. Still, it was not comforting, deep in their shark hearts, to know that they had no true friends.

With the new alliance, the hammerhead image would change radically. All the other important animals down in the deep would see that a respected member of the ocean community, the turtle clan, considered them worthy diplomatic partners. It would be much harder to condemn the hammerheads out of hand—to say it was an affront to decency to have anything to do with them.

While the decision to seek an alliance had been a relatively easy one for the hammerheads, it had been controversial for the loggerhead turtles. The leader of the loggerheads had taken a strictly pragmatic approach. There were many loggerheads who were missing a flipper or a piece of shell because of hammerhead attacks. If an alliance with the sharks meant that those attacks would have to end, wouldn't that be a good thing? But the loggerhead leader's chief rival argued that it was disgraceful for the turtles to lend their prestige to the uncouth and savage hammerheads by favoring them with an alliance. In the end, however, most of the loggerheads, anxious for a respite from hammerhead harassment, had sided with their leader and had approved the alliance.

Following the conclusion of the historic alliance, it would have been easy for the hammerhead sharks simply to congratulate themselves. But not the leader. He said to his fellow sharks, "We must never take things for granted. Down in these treacherous deeps the situation is always fluid. We may feel satisfied for the moment with the success of our diplomacy. But shifting currents can bring sudden catastrophe." The hammerhead leader often delivered his sobering admonitions in dramatic terms, knowing that his fellow hammerheads, conscious of their tremendous strength, were inclined to feel that things must always go their way.

"What exactly," asked one of the hammerheads, "is the danger you foresee?"

"Many of our adversaries," answered the leader, "will certainly be alarmed by this alliance. After all, it increases our power—which they're already scared of. What if the swordfish or the sting-rays secretly approach the turtles and try to persuade them to abandon us and to join them? You will remember that the turtles' decision to join us was not free of controversy in the first place. Will they stick by it? Can we be sure they won't be taken in by slippery promises from others?"

As usual the hammerheads were impressed by their leader's unflinching realism. "What can we do?" they asked.

"I have a plan," declared the hammerhead leader. "We must be sure of getting the maximum warning of any possible defection by the turtles. We will have to know what they are thinking at all times. And we will need to learn about all this just as soon as it happens."

Several hammerheads were skeptical. "That's a tall order. Our hearing may be good—but not that good."

"You see those sucker fish hanging from your stomach?" The leader was referring to the remoras which were attached to many of the sharks. These little fish had suction pads on the top of their heads with which they fastened themselves to the sharks' skin. From time to time they let go in order to grab a few morsels which were scattered in the water when the sharks were feeding.

"As you know," continued the leader, "sucker fish also hang underneath the turtles. So this is what we'll do. We'll get a few of our sucker fish to attach themselves to the turtle leader. They'll be in a position to hear and see everything that goes on. And then they can report to us. They will be perfect spies. The turtles will never know the difference. Who can tell one sucker from the next?"

The plan seemed so sensible and so free of risk that it was immediately put into operation. Seduced by the promise of extra large pickings from shark feasts, two sucker fishes were easily persuaded to serve as spies. One of them would be attached at all times to the bottom of the turtle leader, and they would swim back and forth to the hammerheads in relays so there would never be a time when the activities of the turtle leader were not monitored.

The sucker fish spies performed their mission with great diligence—one might even say brilliance. Reports began to stream in, often twice a day. They mostly concerned turtle tactics for hunting down jellyfish, crabs, and needlefish, the creatures which the turtles found most delectable. This information was of no practical significance to the hammerheads because they, of course, had no interest in such small meals; they went after much bigger fish. Nevertheless, the hammerhead leader insisted that the sucker fish continue to report fully. That was the only way the hammerheads could be certain that the turtles never plotted behind their backs to jettison the alliance.

Then one day information of a completely different order began to arrive. It concerned the sexual lifestyle of the turtle leader. Now it happened that this particular herd of turtles lived by a strict code of sexual ethics. Unlike some other turtle herds, they took their attachments to their marital partners very seriously—bonds often lasting a hundred years. And so it was a matter of exceptional importance when a sucker fish brought in a report revealing that the turtle leader was a philanderer. The report recounted the turtle leader's passionate lovemaking mounted on a ravishingly beautiful female turtle—who was not his spouse. The sucker fish who carried back this information described how he had hung on to the underside of the turtle leader's shell up to the very last second, even though he had risked being crushed. In fact, the sucker fish was later decorated personally by the hammerhead leader for bravery and resourcefulness under unusual circumstances, although this award was naturally kept secret given the fact that it was earned in the course of covert operations.

A second report left little doubt that the leader of the loggerheads was a licentious turtle. It described yet another of his illicit liaisons. And a third report was especially suggestive in light of the first two. It told of the fantastic sexual exploits of the turtle leader's spouse. On one occasion she was mounted by a turtle minister of state and the two of them, coupled together, had floated through the oceans for days enjoying turtle bliss.

The hammerhead leader knew that he had gotten hold of extraordinarily sensitive intelligence. He limited access to it to himself and a few of his closest advisers. These few sharks who were in the know debated when to use this compromising material against the turtle leader. Some thought they should move swiftly to recruit the leader. Then they would have a very highly placed agent who could be counted upon to conduct turtle affairs in a fashion consistent with hammerhead interests.

But others believed the information should be held for some future time of genuine crisis when it might really be vital to twist the flippers of the turtle leader. Premature revelation might jeopardize the sources and methods by which the intelligence had been obtained. Moreover, there was no predicting the reaction of the turtle leader. If he became enraged, the entire alliance might collapse.

The leader of the hammerheads came down on the side of those who favored not making immediate use of their intelligence. Thus, even this spectacular intelligence revealing sexual irregularities joined the vast accumulation of information from which the hammerheads derived no practical benefit. Indeed, so much raw intelligence had been acquired that no individual hammerhead was able to absorb or recall it all. The hammerheads were drowning in information concerning the daily lives and idiosyncracies of loggerhead turtles.

The leader of the hammerhead sharks was well satisfied with the new alliance. True, the turtles had not yet been called upon to show their loyalty to the sharks. But, as the hammerheads had anticipated, their own stature throughout the ocean was rising. It was particularly gratifying to see that they were no longer shunned by those highly respected animals, the porpoises and the dolphins. A rapprochement had even been tentatively broached by a representative of the swordfishes, one of the few creatures whose weapons gave the hammerheads anxiety. And thanks to the tough-minded realism of the hammerhead leader, a massive espionage system against the turtles was functioning smoothly and would provide protection against any wavering in turtle allegiance.

For the loggerhead turtles, the alliance was also producing its intended benefits. The turtles were no longer subject to sporadic assaults from the hammerheads. That, after all, had been the main motivation behind the turtle leader's rather practical alliance policy. For almost all the turtles, the controversy surrounding the original decision had faded from memory.

But for the turtle leader's chief rival for power the issue continued to rankle. He remained obsessed by what he considered a disgraceful abandonment of principle by the turtles in entering into the alliance in the first place. He knew, however, that expostulations against the alliance at a time when the turtles were enjoying its benefits would have been as effective as spitting in the ocean. And so he confined himself to watching and listening and sniffing—hoping that someday something would show up that would be useful to him.

And eventually something did. One day after staring and staring he suddenly became aware that there was something peculiar about the sucker fishes attached to the underside of the turtle leader. These sucker fishes detached and reattached themselves at times which had no connection whatever with whether there were scraps of food in the water to feed on. Even more strange, at those odd times when one sucker fish detached himself a second one always replaced him.

The turtle leader's rival thought and thought but could not figure out any explanation. He could observe no similar sucker fish behavior on the underside of any other turtle. It occurred to the rival that there was only one thing to do. He would follow one of these unusual sucker fish after he had detached himself from the turtle leader.

And so one day the rival turtle began to swim after one of the mysterious sucker fish. It was no easy task. The sucker fish moved in a peculiar fashion. He made sharp and unpredictable turns, accelerating at one point and slowing down at another. In fact, he was practicing the tactics of evasion which he had been taught when he was commissioned as a spy. Nevertheless, the turtle managed to keep the sucker fish in sight, and at last he saw him approach a large school of hammerhead sharks and attach himself to the biggest one of all.

The turtle hovered in the murky ocean background. He observed that a few hammerheads immediately crowded around the big shark—the one who had received the sucker fish—and then after a few minutes the sucker fish detached himself and swam away. The turtle followed him and found that he returned, by a circuitous route, to the loggerhead turtles where he once again attached himself to the turtle leader.

The turtle leader's rival continued his surveillance. And all at once everything fell into place. It dawned upon him that one of the suspicious sucker fish always seemed to depart for his journey to the hammerhead sharks shortly after the turtle leader had held a conference with his senior advisers. The conclusion was inescapable—the turtles had been penetrated by a massive espionage operation controlled by the hammerhead sharks.

The implications of this development were so far-reaching that they took some time to sink into the rival turtle's brain. He knew the turtle leader had tried to be discreet about his amorous adventures—conducting them in inconspicuous spots behind rocks on the ocean floor. Nevertheless the turtles of the herd would be severe in their disapproval, given the high value they placed on loyalty to their spouses. And they would also be displeased by the promiscuousness of the turtle leader's mate. No doubt, the hammerheads were planning to use all this unsavory information to try to coerce the turtle leader into treasonous behavior.

The turtle leader's rival was filled with bitterness—and also with considerable self-satisfaction. He had always known that no good could come of an alliance with sharks. Now he had the evidence to prove that the hammerheads had acted true to form. They had betrayed the trust extended to them. The turtle leader's rival was at last in a position to act decisively. He would confront the leader with evidence of his folly.

But how could he do this without tipping off the hammerheads? A sucker fish spy was always attached to the leader and would immediately report their conversation. Then the rival thought of a stratagem. He sought out a lovely young lady turtle—one who was unusually well-proportioned—and brought her to the leader. The leader was overcome and immediately began to mount her. The sucker fish spy was thereby forced to flee from the underside of the turtle leader to avoid being squashed.

When the spy was out of the way and while the turtle leader was still mounted on the young lady, the leader's rival presented his indictment.

"You fool," he said. "You've jeopardized turtle security. You've subjected us all to the most humiliating invasion of turtle privacy."

"What are you talking about?" responded the astonished leader. "The only invasion of privacy I know about is your attack on me at this singularly inopportune moment. Can't your complaint wait until later?"

"No, it can't," said the turtle rival. "That sucker fish who had to get out of the way so that you could indulge yourself happens to be a spy—an agent of the hammerhead sharks, those bullies you thought we should have an alliance with."

"You're crazy," said the turtle leader.

The leader's rival then recounted how he had conducted his surveillance. When he was finished, the leader was so shaken that he was unable to continue his dalliance with the beautiful turtle.

"We will have to denounce the alliance with the hammerheads," continued the turtle leader's rival. "But before we do so we should secretly seek an alliance with the swordfish so that we'll have some protection against shark retaliation."

The turtle leader was reluctant to take such extreme steps. "What difference does my sex life make anyway? I'll publicly confess my weakness for beautiful lady turtles. And as far as I'm concerned the whole ocean can watch while my wife floats away with other turtles. You see, they won't be able to blackmail me. So where's the big risk to our security?"

"You miss the point," answered the rival. "What the hammerheads have done is an affront to the dignity of the entire turtle herd. Our privacy has been invaded, even if you don't care whether any one knows about your sex life. We extended our trust to the hammerheads, and they treated us with contempt. Our fellow turtles won't stand for it."

The turtle leader, whatever his sexual idiosyncracies, was a realist. It took him only a few seconds to see the magnitude of the impending political disaster. He agreed to his rival's proposals.

"And just one other thing," said the rival. "It is your policy which has failed. Naturally, you will have to resign."

The turtle leader knew he was boxed in. He agreed.

The incoming and outgoing turtle leaders executed their plans without any hitches. The swordfishes were approached secretly and were pleased with the unexpected prospect of supplanting the hammerheads as allies of the loggerhead turtles. The turtles then announced before a representative group of ocean fish that they were withdrawing from the alliance with the hammerhead sharks. They provided a full account of their reasons, stressing the unscrupulousness of the hammerheads.

When the news reached the hammerheads, which it did almost immediately, they were deeply upset. Many were enraged. And, of course, they looked to their leader to formulate a realistic and effective course of action.

"The first thing we must do is issue a categorical denial," said the leader to his followers. "If you assert anything strongly enough, half the fish in the ocean will believe you."

And so a shark spokesman made the following announcement before an assemblage of diverse ocean fish:

"There is absolutely no truth, not one single drop, to the story that hammerhead sharks have spied on their friends and allies, the loggerhead turtles. The charge that they have done so is a malicious fabrication. And besides, as is well known, it is absolutely contrary to hammerhead policy to comment on any of their intelligence operations."

The hammerhead denial did not wash with the vast majority of fish. As accounts of the incident spread throughout the ocean, the hammerheads came to be more despised than ever. Once again they were without friends, and everyone gave them the widest possible berth.

The hammerhead sharks, for their part, did not permit themselves to sulk. Under the direction of their tough-minded leader they conducted a rigorous investigation of the intelligence system which, inexplicably, had let them down and which they therefore knew must be improved.

Although the sharks never discovered how the sucker fish operation had been exposed, they nevertheless remained convinced that there could never be too much effort to increase security through espionage. Next time special intelligence operations were called for they would be more massive than ever. That was the way to be truly hardheaded, a quality which came naturally to the hammerheads.

HEAD-ON COLLISIONS AND OTHER FIASCOS

The Penguins
Who Preserved Their Honor

EVERY DAY AT NOON on a gray windswept island near Antarctica a platoon of about a dozen small penguins marched in formation up a low rocky hill. One after another, with their heads held high and their flippers stretched out to the side, they waddled forward. When they got to the top of the hill, they encountered, invariably, about a dozen cormorants. These big black birds had made their nests there.

The penguins claimed that this advantageous nesting site should be theirs. It was a high spot where water would not wash away eggs. But the cormorants, who had broad powerful wings and sharp beaks, would not move off. When the penguins arrived at the crest of the stony hill, both sets of birds hissed at each other, flapped their wings and flippers, and pecked in the air in each other's direction.

But no beaks made contact. No blood was drawn. And after a few minutes the penguins turned around, placed themselves in formation, and marched down the hill in a dignified fashion. Honor was preserved.

This event occurred every day. Indeed, it had occurred as long as any penguin or any cormorant could remember.

Then things changed. There arrived at the cormorant nesting site a new male, a pugnacious bird who prided himself on never giving quarter in the hard world of bird fights over the ocean.

The new male cormorant was astonished when he observed for the first time the approach of the penguins and their subsequent retreat. He could not contain his indignation as he spoke to the other cormorants. "Why are we playing around with these pen-

guins like this? They are nothing but a nuisance! What we should really do is show them who's boss around here."

The other cormorants were a little embarrassed. They did not want to appear to be sissies before their tough new friend. However, one of the cormorants finally defended their past practice. "What has been the harm? I believe we have established what is known as a *modus vivendi*. As long as we follow this ritual we stay on top of the hill."

"Don't give me a lot of fancy words," answered the male cormorant. "The penguins are obnoxious. They should be taught a lesson. A little humiliation will do them some good."

Next day, the penguins marched solemnly up the rocky hill. At the top they began to hiss and flap and peck in the air as they had always done. But this time the cormorants flung themselves at the penguins with savagery. They bowled the penguins over. They pecked away furiously at their necks and stomachs. Blood flowed.

When the battle was over, the penguins picked themselves up and managed as well as they could to stagger back down the hill. It was a disorderly rout. Not a shred of dignity had been left to the penguins.

Back at the nesting site the new male cormorant did not conceal his satisfaction. "Well, that wasn't so hard, was it?" he demanded of the other cormorants. "That's the last we'll see of those pests."

The following day, at about noon, a formation of penguins waddled up the hill. There was not one line of penguins. There were dozens. They extended hundreds deep. There were brothers, sisters, fathers, grandfathers, first cousins, second cousins, and countless family friends.

The cormorants were overwhelmed. Their nests were trampled over. They fled for their lives.

The penguins took possession of the nesting site. Once again, honor was preserved.

The Camels Who Got
Madder And Madder

A LONG TIME AGO in the Sahara desert there were two herds of wild camels who lived on opposite sides of an oasis. They quarreled frequently about whether one herd or the other was drinking more than its fair share from the pool in the center of the oasis. Shoving matches sometimes got nasty but no one was seriously injured. Then, owing to a severe heat wave—exceptionally bad even for the Sahara desert—the pool began to dry up. As the pool gradually evaporated, the camels got madder and madder. They knocked each other over, kicked viciously, and sat on each other's heads. Their struggle reached its peak when the pool had disappeared entirely—and there was nothing left worth fighting over.

The Cricket Who Stopped The Bombardier Beetles

PFFFFT! A bombardier beetle squirted a scalding spray of poison gas in the face of a small salamander. The salamander staggered a short way and expired. The shiny little beetle crawled through the grass to find another victim. It encountered a grasshopper. Pfffft! A puff of yellow steam pulsed from the beetle's rear end. The grasshopper was engulfed and died quickly.

Pfffft! Pfffft! Pfffft! All through the grass bombardier bullies were exterminating defenseless creatures. Crickets, katydids, grasshoppers, flies, spiders and daddy longlegs—none were safe from the attacking bombardiers who squirted their lethal spray with devastating accuracy.

This dismaying scene was witnessed by a cricket from a secure perch in a nearby tree. The cricket, who was leader of all the crickets in the meadow, was deeply concerned for the survival of his species. Previously the bombardier beetles had only shot their poison at those animals who attacked them. That was fair enough. But now they were going out of their way to find targets and to destroy them. What could possibly explain this frightening shift in bombardier behavior? Where would it all end?

The cricket leader decided to infiltrate a spy into the midst of the bombardier colony. He selected a small brown beetle who resembled the bombardiers and who had been specially trained to behave like them except, of course, that he could not spurt a poison spray. The job was extraordinarily hazardous, for if the brown beetle were exposed the bombardiers would certainly eliminate him.

But in a few days the spy returned safely. And he had a fantastic story to tell. During the night the chief of the bombardiers had held a rally. Elevated on a stone above a writhing mass of thousands of beetles, he delivered a remarkable oration:

"Fellow bombardier beetles, for a hundred million years we have possessed the greatest power on earth—gas! We are superior to all others! We are the supreme race!" The chief then saluted his followers by firing a few volleys of gas into the air. Pfffft! Pfffft! The bombardiers returned the salute. Pfffft! Pfffft! Pfffft!

"With our gas," continued the bombardier chief, "we can exterminate all the weaker creatures of the meadow! They do not deserve to exist! We must eliminate them totally!" Pfffft! Pfffft! The mass of bombardiers was becoming more and more aroused. Pfffft! Pfffft! Pfffft! Pfffft!

"Give me your absolute allegiance and we will triumph!" shouted the chief. "We are the master insects! Bombardiers supreme for another hundred million years! Bombardiers over everyone!" Pfffft! Pfffft! The beetles were in a frenzy. Pfffft! Pfffft! Pfffft! Pfffft! All of them were bent over—poking their rear ends upwards and firing puffs of gas.

The spy was groggy. It was not a nice smell that hung in the air. But he managed to find his way home to the relative safety of cricket headquarters.

The cricket leader called together a small circle of trusted advisers to hear the spy's report and to figure out what to do next. The advisers excelled each other in denouncing the bombardier chief. "Barbaric!" declared one. "Postively uncivilized!" said another. "Utterly uncouth!" cried a third. But no one had practical suggestions. One cricket raised the possibility of negotiation. It was readily acknowledged, however, that anyone who presented himself to the bombardier chief offering to negotiate would probably get a blast of gas in the face.

A few advisers urged that all the creatures of the meadow organize a sustained counterattack against the bombardiers. But then a cricket who had been closely observing the bombardier attacks reported that each beetle appeared able to fire about twenty salvos in a row before exhausting the supply of poison in his tank. With such rapid-fire weapons the bombardiers could mow their attackers down. There would be huge heaps of cricket dead. The advisers were deeply discouraged.

The leader of the crickets then spoke. "There is one practical step we can take." The advisers listened attentively. "Some of you may find my proposal extreme," continued the leader, "but we face desperate circumstances, and now is not the time to be squeamish. I propose that we have the bombardier chief assassinated. He is the inspiration for beetle brutality. To do this job I intend to hire the deadliest of all the insects in the meadow—the assassin bug."

The cricket leader was right to fear the reaction of his colleagues. Indeed, some of them expressed outrage. "What you are proposing," declared one, "is nothing other than political assassination. And that would be to descend to the level of our enemies. I ask you—what will we achieve if we are forced to abandon our moral standards?" Another cricket agreed, exclaiming that to practice political assassination would not be "cricket."

The cricket leader was impatient with his advisers. "What do you think this is—some kind of game? Our way of life may be a few puffs away from extinction. There may be no future cricket generations to carry on all our beloved traditions. These meadows may never ring again with the beautiful sounds of crickets singing. Is that what you want? As the one responsible for our survival I cannot permit myself the luxury of chirping on about what is and isn't cricket."

One adviser persisted in his objections. "And what about the future? Once we do this, there will be no end to cricket leaders deciding to assassinate anyone who happens to irritate them."

"You may be right," conceded the leader. "No doubt there will be crickets who say that what we have done justifies actions that all of us know can't be justified. But that will be up to them. And unless we act to save ourselves now there will be no crickets left to make choices in the future."

Reluctantly the advisers agreed to the leader's plan. But the leader still faced one more obstacle. How could he prevent leaks? A covert operation, like the assassination of the bombardier chief, would surely be wrecked if there was loose chirping about it. And so the leader required that his advisers take the most solemn oath of secrecy.

That evening the leader of the crickets met with an assassin bug. He took extraordinary precautions. The rendezvous took place in a narrow crevice in pitch darkness under a large rock.

After receiving his instructions, the assassin bug made his way toward the bombardier stronghold. In accordance with his special technique, the assassin covered himself with the shells of dead insects. He then moved in short spurts while no one was looking. But most of the time he appeared to be simply a harmless corpse. Finally, having crept up close to the bombardier chief, he pounced upon him, stabbed him with his sharp beak, and sucked out his insides. The bombardier chief ended his existence as an empty shell.

The bombardiers' campaign of terror in the grass quickly collapsed without the fanatical leadership of their chief, and the nightmare of bombardier aggression was over. The crickets danced and sang in celebration. Most thought a miracle had occurred. Only the cricket leader and a few of his most trusted advisers knew the true story. And they could keep a secret.

The Elephants And The Rhinos Who Got Others To Fight Their War

ONCE UPON A TIME on the African plain, long before the present peace between the elephants and the rhinos, tensions between these mighty beasts were unusually high. But neither of them were eager for full-scale hostilities. The consequences could be unpleasant—elephants impaling rhinos with their tusks and rhinos goring elephants with their horns.

One day a rhino had a bright idea. "Let's get someone else to do in the elephants for us," he said to his comrades.

"That's easier said than done," answered another rhino.

"On the contrary," replied the clever rhino, "there'll be nothing to it. We'll get the army ants to harass the elephants. They'll crawl up their trunks and drive them crazy. In exchange, all we'll have to do is promise to protect the ants from the anteaters. The whole operation will be completely risk-free." It was not for nothing that this rhino had acquired a reputation for exceptional craftiness. The other rhinos were delighted and quickly approved the plan.

The ants did as they were bidden, and the elephants soon suffered some terrible provocations. Indeed, several elephants were tortured mercilessly by ant bites high up in their nasal passages. But it did not take long for the elephants to figure out what was happening, especially after they saw the rhinos watching from behind some bushes and heard them snorting with glee.

Most of the elephants were extremely angry and wanted to charge against the rhinos without further ado. But a shrewd old elephant said, "Don't get mad. Get even. Let's round up a gang of anteaters and set them against the ants. We'll offer them support. All we'll have to do, if it ever comes to it, is barge in and stomp out some ants. There won't be any danger at all."

The elephants thought this was a brilliant plan. On reflection they all agreed that the rhinos were not worthy enough opponents to run the risk of incurring serious injury.

Soon a great engagement took place on the plain between a dozen anteaters and several million army ants. It was hard to tell which side was getting the upper hand. At first the anteaters appeared to take a terrible toll on the ants. They had, after all, lots of experience. But then, through sheer numbers the army ants began to overwhelm and tear apart some of the anteaters.

From the sidelines the elephants and the rhinos cheered on their proxies. "Go anteaters! Eat them! Eat them!" shouted the elephants.

"Tear them apart! Kill them! Kill them!" screamed the rhinos.

In fact, the elephants and the rhinos were enjoying themselves immensely. This was certainly better than getting gored in the stomach.

But enthusiasm gradually turned to anxiety. When the elephants saw their friends, the anteaters, dwindle in numbers from twelve to six and then to four, they began to shout, "Enough! Enough! It's time to stop!"

When the rhinos saw their friends, the army ants, shrink from a swirling mass of millions to a few thousands, they screamed, "Stop! Stop! Let's have a cease-fire."

But neither the anteaters nor the army ants paid the least attention. This was not a situation readily susceptible to precise management from the sidelines, or any other sort of fine-tuning. Indeed, forces had been unleashed which had a momentum all their own.

The rhinos said to themselves, "What can we do? If we do not step in, our friends the ants will be exterminated. We promised to help them. We have no choice."

On the elephant side of the arena, a bull said to his comrades, "The situation is desperate for the anteaters. They'll be annihilated if we don't throw our weight on their side. We made a commitment. Our reputation is at stake."

The elephants and the rhinos simultaneously charged in to help their respective clients. They collided head on. In the ensuing struggle almost every one of the mighty behemoths was gored by a tusk or a horn. Many were trampled to death.

It was one of the fiercest conflicts ever witnessed on the African plains. All sides were decimated—the ants, the anteaters, the elephants, and the rhinos.

LEADERS—
RISING AND SINKING
TO THE CHALLENGE

The Chameleon Who Was Rejected And The Brown Lizard Who Was Revered

A CHAMELEON who was prime minister was highly conscientious in trying to reflect the views of the animals whom he governed. Thus, when addressing his subjects he turned black if he thought the prevailing mood was one of anger, yellow if it was one of compassion, and a lovely light blue if faith in the future was the current sentiment. But no progress was made in resolving the really hard problems, such as the explosion in the tiger population. "What's the good," asked the animals, "in having a leader who turns color all the time just to please us but doesn't accomplish anything?"

They threw him out of office.

The next prime minister was not a chameleon, but a lizard whose dull brown scales always remained the same—dull brown. Nevertheless, he was a leader of intense conviction and great persuasiveness. Such was his charisma that when he spoke to his followers about the evils of the jungle, they all turned black with rage. When he described a beautiful future, they became a lovely blue, and when he called for devotion and generosity, they turned to a glowing yellow-orange. For the followers of the lizard it was thrilling to change color frequently. Indeed, for many it was the most gratifying emotional experience of their lives.

The animals gave their enthusiastic support to the brown lizard for many years. It paled into insignificance that no progress at all was made in ameliorating the hard problems of the jungle.

The Leader Who Took
An Unorthodox Treatment

ONCE UPON A TIME the leader of a very important country was nearly beside himself with frustration. He always wanted to do what was right and he knew just what ought to be done, even when everyone else was uncertain. He wanted to take bold initiatives, but these were constantly stalled by his advisers.

They wouldn't let him issue ultimatums because they insisted that it was necessary to think about all the things that might happen if the enemy didn't back down. They dragged their feet when he wanted to offer protection to anyone who stood up to the enemy because they said you could never tell what that might lead to. And when he wanted to cut off allies who weren't staunch enough, they argued that that approach hadn't accomplished much in the past and that alternatives should be considered. It seemed to the leader that his advisers were obsessed with what had and hadn't worked in the past and that they could always think of a million things that could go wrong in the future.

One day, in desperation, the leader decided to respond to an ad in the personal column of a newspaper. "Realize Your Full Potential. Learn How To Surmount All The Obstacles Holding You Back. Achieve Success In Your Chosen Field. Results Guaranteed." And so, departing surreptitiously from his residence during the night, the leader directed his chauffeur to take him to a small storefront in the abandoned part of town where a shriveled old man, who called himself Doctor of Human Engineering, received his clients.

The leader, being an unusually important visitor, was invited into the private room at the rear of the store. The men settled into two tattered armchairs under a bare light bulb which hung by a cord from the ceiling. After telling the doctor about his problems, the leader said, "I am curious, Doctor, what is the method you use to guarantee that people will achieve their goals?"

"As a matter of fact, I sell Microbes."

There was a pause. "Excuse me, I assume you mean prescriptions for—for drugs. That sort of thing. Yes?"

"No! I mean Microbes," answered the doctor. "For example, in your case it would be best for you to take the Wisdom Microbe. I will give you a small test tube filled with a solution of Wisdom Microbes. After you have swallowed them you will be able to reach perfectly balanced judgments. You will know unerringly the soundness of your advisors' objections."

The leader frowned and shook his head. "I'm not sure, Doctor, that you fully understand the problem. Frankly, I'm not all that interested in whether my advisers have perfectly sound opinions. What I want is that their objections shouldn't hold things up. We need to get things done."

"Hmm," muttered the doctor. "Well, I have another idea. If you could look into the future, you would know much better which decisions to push through, wouldn't you? Maybe the best thing for you would be the Foresight Microbe."

Once again the leader shook his head. "Why should I want to see into the future? I might not like what's there. If my decisions get implemented that will be good enough for me. What the people want is decisiveness. We can worry about the consequences later."

There was a long silence. Finally the doctor said, "Well, there is one more possibility. It is a rather extreme remedy. You will have to take not one, but two, Microbes. I have very rarely prescribed this, but in view of the great importance of your position . . ."

"Please, Doctor, let's get on with it."

The doctor then pushed himself out of his armchair and tottered over to a corner of the room where he pulled aside a screen of beads, exposing an old icebox. He removed two test tubes and took them to the leader. He held one up against the bare light bulb.

"Here," he said, "look through this magnifying glass at the solution in the bottom of the tube." The leader saw a large number of tiny spheres, each of which seemed to be encased in a hard smooth shell.

"Nothing can penetrate these little fellows," said the doctor. "You can see that they're perfectly round and slippery. Believe me, nothing can get a grip on them once they're lodged somewhere."

"What are they called?" asked the leader.

"Those are the Ignorance Microbes."

"Ignorance Microbes? I warn you, Doctor, if you're playing some kind of joke on me . . ."

"Wait! Wait! You must see the second Microbe." The doctor held the other test tube up against the dangling light bulb. Once again the leader peered through the magnifying glass. He saw a swarm of tiny creatures who seemed to be bundles of squirming flexing muscles. On their front side, where their chests would have been if they'd had chests, were thick mats of bristling black hair.

"Now those," said the doctor, "are the Willfulness Microbes. Really powerful little guys. But you will have to take both the Ignorance and the Willfulness Microbes together."

"Why is that, Doctor?"

"Well, if you took just one you might wind up very stupid—or just plain obstinate."

"But the Ignorance Microbe! Is that one really necessary?"

"To tell the truth," said the doctor, "not everyone needs both Microbes in equal measure. But I simply cannot guarantee the results unless you take the full combined dose."

The leader looked suspiciously at the doctor. "And just what will happen if I take both?"

"Ahh . . ." sighed the doctor, "there's no telling what you might achieve. The Ignorance and the Willfulness Microbes are the most potent combination in the whole world. Once you've taken both of them, absolutely no one will be able to stop you. You will never be troubled by the failures of the past. When your advisers predict catastrophe you will be able to sweep their arguments aside as nothing but timidity. And when things are really impossible," the old man rose to his feet and began to wave his spindly arms, "you will inspire everyone by urging them to try harder."

"Well, maybe there's something to this," said the leader.

"Just imagine! You can take all your decisions with only one simple rule to guide you. Act First, Think Later."

"Let me have those test tubes, Doctor!" The leader pulled off the corks with twitching fingers. He threw his head back and poured the contents of first one test tube and then the other down his throat.

"I tell you, Doctor," said the leader, "you better be right about what those Microbes are going to do." The two men walked towards the door. The leader completed his thought. "It's not just your reputation that's on the line, Doctor. What's at stake here is the greatness of our country."

The Monkeys
Who Manipulated Matter

ONCE UPON A TIME millions of years ago, a troop of monkeys living in the African forest made a discovery which nearly changed the course of history.

At the time, the monkeys were being harrassed, and occasionally killed, by a band of human beings who had only recently come down from the trees. The humans, who had developed quite a taste for monkey meat, attacked the monkeys with their spears and stone knives. The monkeys resented having to put up with this along with all the customary attacks from leopards, eagles, and pythons.

And so it was that a feeling of considerable exhilaration gripped one of the cleverest monkeys in this unusually intelligent troop when he made his discovery. He found that a special type of mud, if mixed with certain secretions of termites, would become extremely heavy—so much so that when splattered on another animal the mixture would instantaneously penetrate the animal's pores and destroy it.

To impress his peers, the discoverer of heavy-mud conducted a test on a tree frog. He took a tiny blob of the substance and dropped it on the frog's skin. The results were awesome. The brightly colored frog instantaneously disintegrated into a small muddy puddle.

The discoverer of heavy-mud had, of course, told very few other monkeys about his invention since he knew how important it would be to keep the secret from the humans. Nevertheless, rumors had spread rapidly in the troop. The word was getting around that soon, by some miraculous invention, the monkeys would be

completely rid of all of their enemies. There were even wild stories that the obnoxious humans would be reduced to little puddles of mud.

The leader of the troop decided that it was time to take the situation in hand. Some basic decisions were needed. How would heavy-mud be produced? How would it be used? How would the troop be reorganized to carry out its demanding new responsibilities?

The leader convened a meeting of his closest advisers. They huddled together for a whole day in the crown of a tall tree. Taking only short breaks to eat figs, the monkeys pondered over the many dilemmas of heavy-mud policy.

At first, most advisers had seen nothing but opportunity from heavy-mud—to rid themselves forever of all adversaries and especially to do in, once and for all, the humans. But gradually, problems had been raised. Could heavy-mud be safely handled? What if it spilled over some monkeys? How could the discovery be kept secret? The monkeys knew they were extremely loose-lipped. One proponent of heavy-mud suggested that the monkeys would simply have to learn to keep their lips buttoned up. But would it really be possible to transform monkey nature?

Then an older monkey raised even more difficult questions. What if the first attack didn't completely wipe out the humans and then the humans discovered heavy-mud and struck back? Several advisers thought that if others had heavy-mud it would not be so bad in the long run because then nobody would dare to attack anyone else. One ancient adviser even suggested that the monkeys could offer the discovery to others, providing they agreed to an enforceable agreement for jungle peace. But most monkeys thought that was a naive notion. Finally, one monkey who wore a perpetual air of sadness on his face declared it was inevitable that both the monkeys and the humans would obtain heavy-mud and then they would be like two scorpions trapped in a gourd.

The leader had heard enough. He was not a little irritated that the wisest monkeys should have so many conflicting views. He promised to announce his decision the next day.

When the leader returned to his home in a neighboring tree, several females and youngsters greeted him with whoops of delight. It was not often that business kept him away for a whole day.

That evening the leader savored the grooming which he received from his favorite female. He decided to tell her about the decision confronting him. She had already heard rumors of how all the humans would be turned into muddy puddles and was pleased at the prospect. "But what," he asked, "would you think if I told you that the humans might turn our children into muddy puddles?" The leader and his favorite female glanced at the nearest branch where two infant monkeys were squealing and pulling on each other's tails. On another branch some adolescent monkeys were chattering noisily and showing off by doing headstands. The favorite female gazed thoughtfully at her small children. She extended her arm to touch the leader's hand.

Next day, the leader announced his decision to his advisers. He declared that heavy-mud was likely to destroy monkey society long before the humans did. The monkey troop would therefore have nothing to do with heavy-mud. All remaining experimental stocks would be dumped in the deepest part of the river where they could never be recovered. While a few advisers, including the discoverer of heavy-mud, grumbled over the decision, most were relieved and the decision was faithfully implemented.

And that is how it came to pass that early human beings were spared the threat of annihilation by heavy-mud—and had the opportunity over millions of years to develop their own unique discoveries.

The Fish Who Chose
A Magnificent Leader

ONCE UPON A TIME, the ordinary fish in the ocean decided that they should have a leader. The field was narrowed to two candidates: a handsome athletic sailfish and an old sea turtle. A few of the fish thought the turtle should be chosen because his experience over many years gave him wisdom and a sober sense of caution about the great dangers which infested the oceans. He would have sea smarts. But the overwhelming majority of the fish thought the turtle was ugly. And it would be just plain boring to trail after him as he paddled through the oceans.

Almost everyone preferred the sailfish. They admired his magnificent style. With his long sharp sword sticking straight out from his head he could cut through the water faster than any other fish. Even more wonderful, he could leap out of the water, extend the huge sail-like fins on the top of his body and fly through the air above the waves. It would be exhilarating to follow such a leader through the oceans. All the fish would feel good about themselves.

After the sailfish became leader, life did, indeed, become more exciting for most of the fish. They followed him across broad reaches of ocean, through beautiful warm tropical waters and through stormy icy seas. There seemed no limit to how far they could go. And frequently their pride swelled as they looked up and saw on the surface of the water the shadow of their leader flying above the waves.

But it was not equally satisfactory for all the fish. Some, no matter how hard they tried, could not swim fast enough to keep up. These dropouts, abandoned in the great ocean, were easy prey for the sharks.

And sometimes the sailfish led his followers through dangerous waters. Once, in tropical seas, he led the fish into a school of barracuda. These savage hunters tore to pieces a great many of the little fish. Of course, the leader was perfectly safe. He had spent most of the time sailing above the water.

Most fish were at first reluctant to blame their leader. He was, after all, doing what they had elected him to do. He was cutting a magnificent figure, and it was not his fault if the other fish were not as strong or as swift as he was.

Then, one day, while the fish were following their handsome leader through cold northern waters, they suddenly found themselves face to face with a school of killer whales. There was no escape for thousands of fish, who were devoured.

"What's going on?" complained some of the fish who had been lucky enough to survive. "Does our leader know where he's taking us? Does he have any plan for all these excursions?" There were no answers.

"Does he have any idea what's going on below the surface while he's flying high?" asked one of the fish. Still there were no answers.

"And what I want to know," demanded yet another fish, "is whether he really cares about us." Nobody spoke.

"It's time we found the turtle who wanted to be our leader," suggested one of the fish. "He's like us. You can be sure *he* won't fly."

All the fish agreed. They abandoned their magnificent leader. In his place they appointed the turtle.

The sailfish hardly noticed that his followers were gone. He just went on flying safely above the waves.

The Frog Who Put The Blame
Where It Belongs

THERE WAS ONCE a leader of the frogs who was very tough. When
he held talks with their adversaries, the toads, all the other frogs
could be confident he would give nothing away.

Seated on his lily pad, the leader reported to the other frogs: "I began by putting the blame right where it belongs—on the toads. I reminded them that they're eating more than their share of dragonflies, that they've been bullying salamanders, and that they've even spread into parts of the marsh where they don't belong. Most important of all, I held them responsible for inciting the leeches to attack innocent frogs.

"I made perfectly clear," added the frog leader, "that no one desires peace more than we do. And so I said that we want actions—not words. Yes, I told them, your deeds will show if you are serious."

"Unfortunately," the leader continued, "the toads did not respond positively. They did not admit that they were at fault. Instead they recited a long list of accusations against us. They even demanded that *we* prove our good intentions by deeds. And that just goes to show once again that all we're getting from them is words—not actions.

"You can be certain," said the leader, "that the false charges of the toads will get them nowhere. By trying to put all the blame on us, the toads just show that they have no interest in getting down to serious business.

"I am sure you will all agree," concluded the leader, "that we have no choice but to break off these useless talks."

The Caribou Cow
Who Rose To Greatness

MANY YEARS AGO in the barren lands of northern Canada, the leader of a large herd of caribou faced a supreme challenge. One autumn during the annual migration to the south an early and severe winter struck and created the risk that tens of thousands of caribou would perish.

As was customary, an experienced caribou cow led the herd. With her calf trotting close behind her, she marched at the head of a throng of a hundred thousand caribou and made all the crucial decisions during the migration. Should the herd swim across a river swollen by floods? Was the ice thick enough on a lake so that the herd could run across? Or should she lead the herd on a lengthy detour around the lake?

The leader knew that these were life and death decisions. If they were not sound, the herd could break up into smaller groups and that would make it easier for the wolves and bears to attack. The leader therefore formed a caribou council of bulls and cows which she always consulted at critical junctures.

When the herd had been marching south for barely two weeks, the first disaster struck. A fierce blizzard blanketed the land and high winds piled up deep drifts of snow. After temperatures dropped, ice formed over the snow and the caribou had trouble finding lichens and grasses to eat.

Normally the leader charted a somewhat roundabout course to the south to avoid a range of mountains that stood in the way. But when the weather failed to improve and many of the caribou got weaker and weaker from lack of food, she decided that a shortcut over the mountain passes had to be attempted.

As the caribou climbed higher into the mountains, another disaster befell them. The leader took the herd onto a lake which seemed to have a solid cover of ice. But the caribou bunched up and before all could get across, the ice cracked and broke up under the enormous weight. Hundreds of bulls, cows and calves drowned.

Finally, the leader, with a weary herd behind her, approached the narrow rocky pass which would take them downward to safety. But she observed another, smaller herd of animals approaching the pass from a different direction. It was a herd of bighorn sheep. The two herds would meet at the pass at about the same time and only a single file of animals would be able to march through.

The leader met with her council. "How shall we proceed?" she asked. "Who will go first through the pass?"

"We must go first," answered a large bull. "We are much stronger in numbers. The sheep must defer to us."

"But what if they choose to fight?" asked a cow on the council. "This is bighorn territory and they may fight fiercely."

"We will still prevail," said another bull. "We will wear them down. And a victory now will greatly lift the morale of the herd."

"In fact," said a third bull, "the sheep should be able to understand this and they should accede to our demand."

The leader was annoyed with the bulls. During the arduous trek, they had done nothing to curb their battles, which accompanied the breeding season. Many fine males had killed and maimed each other. The injured bulls had quickly fallen prey to bears and wolves. Why hadn't the bulls been able to see that this year it was much more important to preserve every bit of the herd's strength than to play their competitive games? And now the bulls were proposing ultimatums and more fighting.

The leader turned to survey her herd. They had endured extraordinary hardships. Over half of the yearlings had perished from drowning or attacks by wolves and grizzlies. Her own calf standing by her side was clearly on his last legs. What good would more fighting do? And there was every reason to expect the bighorns to fight. If the caribou went through the pass first, moving in single file as they would have to, it would be days before the bighorns could resume their journey. All that time the bighorns would be subject to attack by wolves.

The leader announced her decision to the thousands of waiting caribou. The bighorns would be invited to merge with the caribou towards the head of the line; everyone would move through the pass in single file.

The leader next approached the herd of bighorn sheep. Like the caribou herd, they were in a state of exhaustion from cold and hunger. She conveyed her proposal to the leader of the bighorns, who gratefully accepted it.

All went smoothly as the caribou and the bighorns filed through the pass. Moreover, the caribou received an unanticipated benefit. The bighorns, who knew the mountainous terrain well, served as scouts for the caribou. The bighorns scampered to nearby ridges where they could spot wolves or grizzlies from a distance. They guided the caribou along the safest and quickest path to the southern forest, saving many days of travel and preserving thousands of caribou lives.

Many years later, the statesmanship of the caribou leader was chronicled by the great caribou historian Thucydibou. He recorded her oration before the caribou throng. Her words have since become famous:

"We make our friends not by demanding favors but by doing them."

LEARNING
AND
MISLEARNING

The Serpent Who Enticed
The Homo Sapiens

ONE DAY many thousands of years ago a Serpent deep down in the bowels of the earth felt some strange stirrings. He knew that the time had come to fulfill his destiny. And so he climbed up and up and slithered out of his hole. Now he realized that he was supposed to approach one of those animals known as primates but he was a little vague about just which one. So the first creature he hailed was a Small Monkey.

"My friend," said the Serpent, "I have an extremely important proposition for you."

The Small Monkey was suspicious, but also a little curious. "What I'd like," continued the Serpent, "is to see you become the most powerful monkey in the whole jungle. All you have to do is this. Just let everyone else know that you have the finest morals in the whole world. Then insist that all other monkeys behave strictly in accord with your standards. That's all you have to do. And if you're conscientious about it, I'll use my special powers to see to it that you become the supreme monkey."

The Small Monkey could smell that something was not quite right. "Why," he asked, "should I want to be the supreme monkey? What I really want is to find enough good fruit for me and my troop. And when we're not hiding from eagles, I'm happy to enjoy a good grooming from one of my wives. No, I don't think enforcing morality is really for me."

The Serpent slithered away hoping to find a weightier creature. He soon encountered a Gorilla.

"Just a minute," said the Serpent. "You, sir, are really lucky that our paths have crossed. It so happens that I have a secret that will

make you the most powerful Gorilla in the world. Here's what you need to do. Use your strength to promote righteousness. Just tear apart any other ape who won't praise your virtue and acknowledge the wisdom of all your pronouncements."

The Big Gorilla directed a black frown at the Serpent. "Why should I bother myself with righteousness? I've got some real problems. This arthritis in my hip is killing me." The Gorilla was not one to waste words. He limped off into the jungle.

The Serpent was discouraged. He'd made two tries to do what he was supposed to. That was all that could be expected. So he began his journey back to his hole. But just before he got there he spied a strange creature. The Serpent decided he had better be polite. Who could tell what might come of the encounter?

"My dear sir," said the Serpent in his most ingratiating manner, "I don't believe I've had the privilege of making your acquaintance. May I inquire who you are?"

"I," announced the creature, not without a trace of pride, "am Homo Sapiens."

The Serpent was not very impressed. He noticed that the creature had very little hair on his body and compared to the Gorilla he was decidedly skinny. It would have been much better if that magnificent Gorilla had been interested in his proposition. But at this point how could the Serpent be fussy?

"Well, my friend," said the Serpent, "I congratulate you on your good fortune. It just may be that I can do something pretty special for you. How would you like to be the greatest Homo Sapiens in the world?" The Serpent saw the eyes of the strange creature light up. Maybe there was real potential here.

"You won't have to do anything very difficult or unpleasant," said the Serpent smoothly. "I assume you possess moral standards. And surely they are superior to everyone else's." The Serpent paused and the Homo Sapiens nodded immediately. "Just insist," continued the Serpent, "that everyone—absolutely everyone—comply strictly with your excellent standards."

"That's an intriguing idea," replied the Homo Sapiens. "I must confess it has a certain basic appeal. You know, I've had a feeling that I'm destined for greatness." The Homo Sapiens began to comb his fingers through the tangle of matted hair which hung from his face.

"Well, if I'm going to help you accomplish great things," said the Serpent, "I must be frank. I hope you don't mind my saying this, but you seem to be a little on the puny side. Mind you, that's nothing to be ashamed of. You're just not an elephant or a gorilla. But to play your true role you're going to need a lot more muscle. And that's where I come in. If you do just what I say, I'll use my special powers to see that you have very great strength. You'll be the master of things that fly through the air, things that explode, things that burn with amazing heat, things that nobody ever dreamed of."

The Homo Sapiens could hardly comprehend such vast possibilities. After a moment of silence he spoke again. "Tell me," he asked, "how will I know when to use this great power?"

"Very simple," answered the Serpent. "You have to learn one rule. Just one. It is this. There Is Only One Right Way."

The Serpent paused to let his words sink in. "You must permit no deviations, no lapses by anyone, no dissents. And you must never hesitate to use whatever force is necessary to demonstrate that you are entirely in the right."

"Wait a minute," said the Homo Sapiens. "Isn't there some danger for me? What if someone else thinks they're right also, and he's so obstinate that he fights me?"

"Well, that's exactly the point," answered the Serpent. "That's why you must always fight and win. If someone defeats you, that will prove that he was right and you were wrong. That's why your strength must be greater than anyone else's."

"But what happens," asked the Homo Sapiens, "when I've proved that I'm stronger than everyone else? What will I do then?"

"Ah, a very intelligent question," said the Serpent. He wanted to encourage this promising disciple. "When you have become stronger than anyone else, you can demonstrate your moral superiority by many ways other than fighting. You can hold trials. You can insist on confessions. You can render verdicts. You can even demonstate your power by issuing pardons when your opponents confess their errors. Have no fear, there will never be an end to your job."

"Well," declared the Homo Sapiens, "the more I hear about this proposition, the more I like it."

The Serpent said nothing. He sensed that they had reached the critical point of the interview. He betrayed only the slightest increase in excitement as his tongue, with its two pointed ends, flicked in and out of his mouth a little more rapidly than normal.

"Okay! I'll do it!" declared the Homo Sapiens. His eyes glittered. "Yes, I'm ready. Ready to go! I'll rush back to my clan and I'll issue my first law. Practice What I Preach!"

"Good thinking," interjected the Serpent.

The Homo Sapiens ran off in a high state of exhilaration. His shouting could be heard for some distance. "One Right Way! One Right Way!"

The Serpent slithered back down into his hole. He would never know all the details of what would ensue over the millennia to come. Crusades, scorched earth, sieges, blockades, thirty-year wars, hundred-year wars, raids, reprisals, invasions, blitzkriegs, holocausts, world wars, regional wars, jihads, pacifications, interventions, massacres, highjackings, pre-emptive attacks, surgical strikes—Homo Sapiens would always know he was in the right.

The Snow Monkeys
Who Achieved Tranquillity

ONCE UPON A TIME on an island north of Japan there lived a troop of snow monkeys. Every winter these monkeys endured blizzards and gales. It was so cold that the snow which matted on their coats of fur often turned to ice. The monkeys could not even enjoy the pleasure of grooming each other.

Everyone was always exhausted. In single file the monkeys would trudge through deep snow up and down steep mountains. They were looking for trees which had bark that could be scratched off and chewed on. Almost every winter one or two older monkeys would fail to survive till spring.

One winter everything changed. The monkeys came upon a pond which, strangely, was not covered by ice. Even more strangely, mist and steam swirled over the surface of the water. A young snow monkey who was more adventurous than his elders dipped his toe into the water. Then his ankle. And then he eased his whole shivering body into the delicious warmth. When the other monkeys saw the rapturous expression on his face, they all followed his example.

Soon monkey life was centered on the thermal pool. They spent hours with only their heads above the water. Complexions turned from blue to pink. Grooming and making love again became enjoyable all year around.

Not long after this wonderful turn of events, the blissful tranquillity of the monkeys was roughly jolted. One day there suddenly appeared near the edge of the pool a large brown bear. He was very fierce. And he was hungry, too. Standing on his hind legs, he growled and roared, and pawed the air with his claws. Then he approached the water.

The monkeys rushed out of their baths and confronted the bear at the edge of the pool. They shrieked and bared their teeth and jumped up and down. Their frenetic behavior so shocked the bear that he retreated. The monkeys returned to their immersion in the warm waters.

But the bear, who remained hungry, came back. And the whole scene of wild activity was re-enacted. Not once, but many times. Soon the monkeys were as weak and exhausted as they had ever been.

The young monkey who had discovered the thermal pool then had an idea. He said to his fellow monkeys, "When the bear approaches next, stay where you are in the pond. Do not rush out of the water to scare the bear away."

"Are you crazy?" shouted an older monkey. "We will all be attacked and eaten!"

"Please, do what I say," pleaded the young snow monkey.

Normally, it would have been presumptuous for a junior monkey to offer such advice, and the senior monkeys would have rejected it out of hand. But everyone was tired and at their wits end.

Once again the bear approached. He bellowed and roared. Un-opposed, he charged into the water toward the monkeys who huddled together on the far side of the pond. As the bear waded in deeper, his roars turned into grunts. Then he slowed down. In the middle of the pond he stopped altogether. With just his head above the steaming water, he breathed deeply and sighed contentedly. A smile settled on his face and his eyes slowly closed.

And that is how it happened that some snow monkeys and a fierce brown bear came to coexist peacefully in the snowy mountains of an island north of Japan.

The Rattlesnake Who Explained His Behavior

A HUMAN BEING who happened to be a leader of worldwide renown found himself exhausted after a week of critical state business. He had formulated plans for armed intervention in an underdeveloped country, given approval for weapons sales to opposing factions in a civil war, and authorized the bombardment of a recalcitrant nation in order to foster negotiations. Seeking some relaxation so that he might be fresh for the next week's endeavors, the statesman repaired to his mountain retreat.

While strolling along a forest path, the statesman observed a conflict between two rattlesnakes. After shaking their rattles, the two snakes began to wrestle. With their bodies entwined, they strained and pushed against each other. At last one of the rattlesnakes pinned the other to the ground and the defeated snake slithered off. Said the statesman to the victorious rattlesnake:

"I am impressed with your skill at wrestling. But if I'm not mistaken your venom can kill other rattlesnakes. Why didn't you just bite your enemy and finish him off?"

"Are you serious?" answered the snake. "Why should I kill one of my own kind? Rattlesnakes are civilized animals."

The Fish Who Brought
Light To The Abyss

DEEP IN THE ABYSS near the ocean floor there lived a community of little fish who carried around with them their own lights. There was a female angler fish, who had a long thin rod extending up from her head at the end of which dangled a small glowing bulb. There were a few lantern fish. They had headlights which shone out of their eyes. And there were several hatchet fish. They carried rows of lights on their stomachs. These fish were all quite proud of their achievement. They were not very powerful, these lights. But still, they had brought some small patches of illumination to a place which otherwise would be perpetually dark.

The domain of the little fish with lights was invaded one day (it might have been one night—who could tell?) by a gang of fish without lights. These were pretty ugly and uncouth customers, at least in the opinion of the fish with lights. They were gulper fish who had enormous jaws and sacklike bodies which could receive anything they happened to ingest. There was also an oarfish, a very long creature with a long flat tail. The oarfish swam around just above the primeval ooze, twisting this way and that.

The fish with lights did not much like these primitive intruders. They were particularly upset because the oarfish had also brought with him a retinue of tiny herrings. Those small beings were entirely dependent on the big oarfish. They fed on the scraps which fell from the oarfish's jaws as he snaked his way through the water.

The fish with lights complained among themselves that no one, not even a great oarfish, had the right to acquire a string of satellite fish and then keep them in the dark. A lantern fish commented that the oarfish probably wanted all those herrings trailing after him because if another fish sneaked up to attack him the herrings would get eaten first. In the opinion of the fish with lights, this was intolerable. The water belonged to everyone and all fish should be free from domination. They should demand, said the angler fish, that the oarfish give up his retinue and let the herrings live their own lives.

When the oarfish heard this proposition, he told the fish with lights to mind their own business. He warned that if anyone interfered with him or his herrings he would react harshly. The fish with lights refused to be intimidated. They believed the oarfish was just bluffing. The angler fish was particularly indignant. She knew that she and her friends were in the right. Had they not brought light to the abyss? Civilization on the ocean floor was at stake. A lantern fish suggested that they should all swim around the oarfish and direct their lights toward him. The herrings would surely be lured away. And the oarfish would see that the power of light was greater than the power of darkness.

The fish with lights proceeded to execute their plan. As anticipated, the herrings were attracted to the light and left the oarfish. And, as he had promised, the oarfish retaliated swiftly. He inserted his long flat tail into the ooze which blanketed the ocean bottom and twisted with all his might. He soon stirred up a tremendous cloud of mud. No lights could penetrate this ooze. Not the tiny light hanging above the head of the angler fish. Not the headlights of the lantern fish. Not the row of pale lights on the stomachs of the hatchet fish. The fish with lights were now truly in the dark.

A little above the mud cloud a hungry gulper fish sensed that something peculiar was going on below. He descended with his enormous jaws stretched wide. The fish with lights would normally have seen the gulper coming. But that was now impossible.

And so the gulper ingested the angler fish, then the hatchet fish, and then the lantern fish. All were thrown back into the big sack behind the gulper's head.

The angler fish declared to her friends, who were squeezed next to her, "We were entirely in the right."

"Yes," said a lantern fish. "But sometimes you can be right—but wrong."

And the digestive juices of the gulper began to flow.

The Cat Who Gave A Special Gift

ONCE UPON A TIME there lived together, that is to say, under the same roof, a leading statesman and a cat of profound imperturbability. Their mutual rapport was so great that it might be said that each belonged to the other.

Over the years the cat had spent a good part of her life in contemplation and analysis. For hours she would squat on her haunches by the little round window in the attic of the statesman's mansion, which was high on a hill, and survey the panorama of human activities in the capital below. Then when there were meetings of all the government ministers in the ornate cabinet room, the cat would occupy her special space in a large bowl on a sideboard and, with her head peeking over the rim, she would patiently take everything in. Even in the war room where the statesman and the generals and admirals argued about what to do in impending crises, the cat had her unobtrusive perch—behind a little opening in the wall from which a slide projector occasionally flashed the strategic situation onto a screen.

Now this cat was no dummy. And so, using her native shrewdness, she acquired a vast reservoir of wisdom about the conduct of state business. Over the years, however, as she got older and more mature she became increasingly disquieted. It seemed to her that affairs of state had gotten more and more frenetic, less and less productive, frequently ludicrous, and sometimes downright dangerous.

Day after day she observed ministers arguing with each other and seldom reaching decisions. She heard officials describing some sort of glorious past and blaming each other for its loss. At diplomatic meetings with foreign representatives, which she moni-

91

tored from atop a nearby bookcase, she saw that persons who clearly considered themselves important were fond of wasting an amazing number of words. And what was even stranger, they seemed to make demands and issue threats and then never do anything about them.

One thing she found particularly puzzling was what the humans called "war." It was one thing to have an occasional scrap and come away with a few scratches. But what was going on when thousands of these humans went around throwing terrible firecrackers at each other? Peering from her small attic window with those keen eyes of hers she had observed ships come into the harbor and humans carried horizontally on sheets into vehicles. How were such persons going to enjoy their fish and their steaks? If that's what war did to humans, who needed it?

As the cat reached old age she realized what an excellent life she had led in the statesman's home. In her youth she had spent much time outdoors climbing large old oak trees on the grounds and chasing birds. Within the mansion, many special privileges had been accorded to her. She had not been forced to take her meals downstairs in the pantry with a couple of uncouth and slovenly dogs. She dined upstairs in the statesman's study, often eating the same dishes he did—filet of sole, salmon steak, and boeuf bourguignon. Then, afterwards, near the fire, while he read state papers, she often curled up in his lap, and late at night, when nobody was likely to interrupt, they conversed. For the cat it had been a life of constant enrichment.

Now she wanted to show her gratitude to her dear friend before old age left her feeble in body and mind. It was not easy to think of a suitable gift. The statesman seemed to have everything. At one point she resolved to catch for him several tender young birds to be roasted, but then she felt a little uncertain, never having seen him eat sparrows. Perhaps it would be better to give him something that might help with his work—make him a truly superior statesman. But what would such a gift be? Finally, after many days and nights of quiet concentration she had the answer.

And so late one evening when she was ensconced in the statesman's lap she said in a barely audible purring voice, "I am getting old. Before I go, I would like to do something for you."

"There's no need for that," answered the statesman. "Sharing your company has been quite enough for me."

"Well, I insist," said the cat. "I want to help you become the world's most excellent statesman."

"All right," the statesman replied. He had long ago learned not to argue with her. "I will be very happy to accept your gift."

The cat then jumped down to the carpet. Sitting on her haunches she said, still with a purring voice but a little more firmly, "Now, please get your pad and a pen and take down what I say."

The statesman did as he was bidden. The cat began to dictate. "Memorandum. Subject: Pointers To Achieve Masterly Statesmanship." The cat had often listened as the statesman had dictated his own memoranda to his secretary, and so she had become familiar with all the appropriate stylistic requirements.

"Introduction," continued the cat. "The following guidelines are based upon my unblinking observation of the human scene. I wish to set them down not because I desire to improve the dignity and equilibrium of human beings—that may be beyond anyone's capacity—but because I am most eager to assist my dear friend to achieve the highest honors in his profession."

The cat paused. Slowly she lifted her paw and then scratched behind her ear. "Now where shall I begin?—No, don't take that down!" Suddenly there was a trace of bossiness in her soft voice. "I was just thinking. All right. Begin! Point one. How to Avoid Mistakes. The Need for Greater Caution. You must never rush to accept a proposal—no, pounce—make that, you must never pounce upon a proposal. Always stare, watch, wait and stare some more. And after that, give the idea a very good sniffing—feel it over with your whiskers—correction, please. Make that—with your mustache."

The statesman was scribbling furiously. "Am I going too fast for you?" asked the cat. "No, I've got it all down," answered the statesman.

"Good. Now, point two. Maintaining a Proper Perspective. You must permit yourself to get agitated only about really important things. Surely you can put up with quite a bit, and maintain considerable poise, if you know that you'll soon be enjoying a really good meal—like fish with lots of cream sauce.

"Next. Point three. Conflicts. Never get into a fight if you can avoid one. If you can be upstairs and the dog stays downstairs, what's wrong with that?

"Point four. No. Correction. Continue with point three. Of

course, if you can't avoid a confrontation, by all means arch your back and flatten your ears. But allow a few moments to pass before you strike. Who knows what fleeting thoughts may distract your adversary, like the aroma of a fine female. He may stalk off—and no one will have been scratched at all.

"Point five—"

"You haven't given me point four yet."

"Well, you can straighten it all out when you transcribe your notes," said the cat with an edge of peremptoriness. "Next point. How should you size up your opponent? You humans shouldn't be so obsessed by size. We cats know that some of the biggest creatures are the clumsiest. And then you must not forget about taking into account the—how do you say it?—the psychology?— Yes, the psychology of your adversary. He may be big but soft. Who wouldn't rather run into a human being than, say, a dog? Have you got all that?"

"Yes, certainly."

"Now, point five, I believe. How to Conduct Diplomatic Intercourse. First of all, you should be much more careful what you complain about. Anyone with self-respect, whether he or she has four legs or two, must understand that to call something 'intolerable' when you may have to tolerate it later can only lead to mortification."

"Yes, yes," mumbled the statesman, who was becoming quite absorbed with taking the dictation, "that's a powerful point."

"If I may continue," said the cat, "it is essential that humans maintain greater composure in their political and diplomatic affairs. Raucous and hectoring delivery of points is always most unimpressive. Speak in a soft purring voice—so soft that others must concentrate to listen. If you speak softly enough your vis-a-vis will think he is being entrusted with secrets—which is, of course, very flattering. You might, at crucial moments, emit a silent miaow."

The cat let out a deep breath. "I must say this is more exhausting than I anticipated. Let's take a milk break." The statesman did what was expected of him. He went downstairs and returned with a bowl of warm milk and hot cocoa for himself. A few minutes later, when both were refreshed, the cat resumed her dictation.

"All right. Next point, whatever number it is. Firmness and

Friendship. Yes, you must always keep sharp claws—just in case a scrap cannot be avoided. But I have always found that much can be achieved through friendly gestures toward important parties. I would suggest a good lick on the face for those who are not enemies.

"Now I have only one more point—a rather delicate one. On the immaturity of humans. You will agree, I have no doubt, that I am unusually well qualified to speak on the subject of maturity—having reached the age of twenty-three."

"Excuse me," interrupted the statesman. "Is that part of the dictation?"

"No. I am collecting my thoughts. It is an extremely difficult subject for me to speak about. We cats are fully mature from a very early age and it does not come easily to understand why so many of the two-legged creatures never grow up. I have been reflecting on the question for a long time.

"All right. Begin the dictation. Last point. Maturity. For everyone's sake, humans must learn to take things a little easier. You talk a lot about keeping your cool, but you don't do it. Above all, you must stop trying to prove things all the time. And who knows what you're trying to prove anyway? That you never blink? That you can stand up to anyone? That you know what's best for everybody else? And why do you have to prove these things over and over again? It is really so tedious!

"The truth," continued the cat, "is so clear that anyone can see it—even in the dark. You are trying to prove these things all the time because you have not grown up enough to know who you are. I would suggest, with all modesty, that you emulate cats. We know who we are. We are not trying to show that we are as strong as horses or that we can fly like pigeons or swim like ducks. We are completely comfortable being cats."

The cat's purring voice got softer and softer. The statesman had to concentrate very hard to make out all her words. "You will be mature," whispered the cat, "when you know who you are—and when you stop trying to be lions, eagles or bears."

There was a long pause. "And now I am through," said the cat. She gave herself a good stretch. Then she walked slowly to her basket, stepped in, curled herself up and went to sleep.

It was not long afterwards that she breathed her last. She was

found lying under a bush in the garden. Understandably the statesman was deeply saddened. He buried her in the garden.

The statesman told no one of the unusual bequest which his cat
had made to him. He knew that others would scoff at such a
document. But he studied it often—even after he came to be
recognized as the preeminent statesman of his time.

SAD EVENTS

The Lamb Who Imitated The Lion

THE LION, who ruled the animal kingdom, ate a different one of his subjects every day. Sometimes it was a pig, sometimes a deer— and occasionally he ate a chicken if he wanted a snack. No one complained. This was the way things had always been.

One day a lamb, having observed the behavior of the lion, marched up to a chicken, kicked her senseless, and ate her.

The other animals were outraged. They put the lamb to death— for challenging the established social order.

The Elephant Who Fixed Things Up

ONCE UPON A TIME a snail set out to find an elephant. After a lengthy journey—a really arduous effort for the snail—he came upon a huge bull elephant who was browsing with his wife.

"Sir," said the snail gazing way up, "my friends and I find ourselves in a very difficult situation. We need your help. In fact, we are at our wit's end."

"Tell me what's wrong," said the elephant. "And just who are these friends that you speak of?"

"Well," answered the snail, "we all live under a large flat rock, and things aren't going so well there. All my friends—the woodlice, the roaches, the mites, the worms and the slugs—we normally get along fine under the rock, but now there's something we just can't cope with. The situation is crushing us."

"Please don't meander," said the elephant. "Come to the point!"

"There's a very big beetle down there, and he's bossing everyone around. He's a real dictator—Big Beetle. If you don't do exactly what he wants, like dig tunnels for him, he bites your head off."

"I see," said the elephant. "Why don't you all just leave?"

"But why should we? We would be abandoning our home. And it's a pretty nice home—dark, and full of special aromas."

"Is there no talking to Big Beetle?" asked the elephant. "Can't you persuade him to be more—more moderate?"

"We've tried," said the snail, "but Big Beetle says that anyone who complains is being insubordinate and—snap—off comes another head."

"Yes, I begin to visualize the situation under that flat rock. You don't seem to have much room for maneuver." The elephant paused for a moment. "And why, if I may ask, were you the one chosen to go out and find help?"

"Well," answered the snail, "as you know, I have something that protects me from the sun—my shell. I can go anywhere. The others were naturally afraid that if they came out from under the rock they might dry up."

"So, what makes you think I can be of help?" asked the elephant.

"We thought you would be sympathetic. You're free and independent. You know what it means not to be bullied. And, of course, you have the strength to deal with a beetle."

The elephant thought for a moment. "Yes, it is true. We elephants know the value of freedom. And you are quite right, this petty tyrant—Big Beetle—will be no match for me."

Now the bull elephant's spouse, although not participating in the conversation, had been listening carefully. Finally she was moved to interject herself. "Wait a minute, Great Bull!" She used his familiar nickname. "You may be strong, and you may even be savvy in the ways of elephants. But just how much, if it is not too much to ask, do you know about woodlice, mites, slugs and worms? Things may not be so simple down there under that flat rock. Are you sure you know enough to take this job on?"

"What should be so hard about straightening things out for a few worms?" answered the bull elephant. "Those little animals just want to live their lives in freedom and dignity the same way we do. What's so complicated about that?"

"And what, specifically," demanded Great Bull's spouse, "do you propose to do when you get to the flat rock?"

"Don't worry about that," answered Great Bull. "I will think of something. We elephants are nothing if not resourceful. And besides, I have a duty to assist. How can a great and privileged animal, like myself, fail to heed a call for help from lesser creatures who are not so fortunate? You can rest assured, everything I do will be in the best interests of those poor little animals."

Great Bull then turned to the snail. "Come, let us be on our way." He delicately picked up the snail in the tip of his trunk and stuck him on his forehead. From that vantage point, the snail guided Great Bull back to the large flat rock.

When they arrived, Great Bull put the snail back down on the ground. He then stared long and hard at the top of the rock. "Tell me again," he said to the snail. "what's going on underneath?"

And so once more the snail described for Great Bull all the indignities, the frustrations and the injustices that were suffered by the little animals at the hands of Big Beetle.

"Hmm, well," muttered Great Bull, "I don't see evidence of something wrong. The rock isn't shaking or anything. Are you sure that all that you say is going on?"

"Yes, certainly," replied the snail. "I have spent most of my life down under that rock."

There was another long pause. Finally Great Bull said, "All right, what we need here is decisive action." Great Bull began shifting his tremendous bulk from side to side, pushing down on the enormous pads which were his feet. "It's no good taking little steps. There has to be a quick and bold solution." He was breathing heavily. "What's needed is, well—an upheaval!"

And with that Big Bull wedged his truck under the edge of the large flat rock, gave forth a tremendous roar and, with a mighty heave, overturned the rock.

When Great Bull recovered from his exertion he looked down and began bellowing, "Where's Big Beetle? Where's Big Beetle? I'm going to teach him a thing or two!" Great Bull curled his trunk and lowered his head. He soon spied a large black beetle scurrying in the grass. The elephant then reared up and crashed down with one of his front feet landing exactly where the black beetle was.

"Hah! That's it for Big Beetle!" shouted Great Bull triumphantly. He looked around and saw that the snail had not gone very far. "Well, my little friend," said the elephant, "that takes care of that!" He then sauntered off toward his home. His stride had a little more bounce than usual, and a deep humming came from his huge head.

In the meantime the little animals, who had been suddenly exposed to the sunlight by the elephant's decisive action, did what their instincts demanded. They searched frantically for another large flat rock, and they found one not too far away.

Those animals who managed, before they were cooked, to get under the new rock realized immediately that this space was not unoccupied. There were, of course, worms, mites, roaches and woodlice. And under one corner of the rock there was also a nest of yellow jackets.

The little animals soon encountered their new boss. His name was Big Yellow Jacket.

The Rats Who Were Trapped

FOR OVER a hundred years two communities of rats waged a war in an old abandoned tenement. The brown rats lived in the cellar, the black rats in the attic, and their struggle took place in the wasteland between them.

Now after every engagement, no matter which side came out ahead, each pack of rats held its own ceremonies to honor those who were killed. The rats became inebriated, nibbling side by side on fermented garbage. In their squeaky voices they sang sad ballads recounting ancient injustices. From bits of debris they molded statues of the dead martyrs.

And then it came to pass that the black rats achieved a great victory. Using choice garbage as a lure they ambushed the large, clumsier brown rats on the half-collapsed stairs which separated the two territories. They inflicted on the brown rats terrible casualties, the heaviest in many years. Clearly the leader of the black rats was a military genius.

All of a sudden the leader was seized by a vision. He foresaw a brighter future for the rats. And so, after the great victory, he asked himself whether he should not begin negotiations for peace. Would there ever be a better time than when the enemy was reeling from a setback? He told the other black rats about his idea.

The black rats were shocked. How could any leader have forgotten the sacrifices of so many brave rats over the past hundred years? What right did any rat have, even if he was a military genius, to prevent the rats of future generations from giving their lives and becoming martyrs? In whose honor would future rats carve statues? Or sing ballads?

They convinced their leader that he had momentarily lost sight of what was truly important.

That night the black rats ate a lot of fermented garbage. They pledged that they would never abandon the struggle until they had avenged the death of every black rat—by destruction of every brown rat. And then they sang all the beautiful old songs.

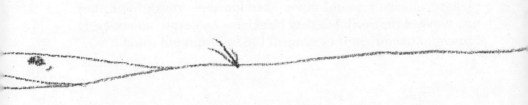

The Woolly Rhinoceros
Who Was Determined To
Reverse His Fortunes

A LONG, long time ago, when snow and ice covered much of the
Northern Hemisphere, it occurred to a Fox that during all his
travels across the tundra he had come upon only one Woolly
Rhinoceros.

What the Fox saw was a solitary figure—the craggy bulk of a
Rhinoceros standing out starkly against the gray arctic sky. Occasionally the Rhinoceros would wheel around suddenly as if startled
by something. An insect? A mouse? Or was he stirred by some
distant memory? Sometimes the Fox saw clouds of steam burst
from the Rhinoceros's nostrils. Was the Fox being too fanciful

when he wondered if this beast had once been driven by great passions? Could the Woolly Rhinoceros be the possessor of a strange and terrible past?

One thing especially bothered the Fox. Where was the Rhinoceros's spouse? Where were his friends? Why were there no baby rhinos? And why was there no herd of Woolly Rhinoceroses? The Fox was baffled.

Then one day the Fox had an idea. Could it be that there really were no more Woolly Rhinoceroses? Was it conceivable that this great shaggy creature was the last surviving Woolly Rhinoceros in the world?

The Fox became determined to learn the true story. But he would have to be careful. The Rhinoceros was reputed to be highly irascible. Not a few smaller animals had come to grief on his sharp front horn when they had failed to keep their proper distance. And so the Fox approached the great Woolly Rhinoceros with caution. When he was within earshot, the Fox ventured these words:

"Esteemed neighbor, I beg leave to approach you and to present a most unusual request." The Woolly Rhinoceros glowered at the Fox and said nothing.

"I have embarked on a project of far-reaching importance," continued the Fox, "and your participation is essential for its success."

"What project?" grunted the Woolly Rhinoceros.

"I am preparing an Oral History of the Ice Age. An interview with you will be vital in making it possible for everyone to understand the momentous events of our era. My Oral History will be passed down from generation to generation. It is bound to have a profound impact on many great animals."

The Woolly Rhinoceros, despite himself, was flattered and agreed. The interview began early in the morning as a cold white sun low on the horizon shimmered over the snowy tundra. The two animals huddled behind a small hillock taking shelter from the gusts of arctic wind.

"Well," said the Fox, "let's start back a little when times must have been much better. I suppose there were once a lot of Woolly Rhinoceroses on the tundra?"

"Oh, yes, more than you could count. We were a very large

herd—and I was the leader," said the Rhinoceros with not a little pride. "Those were wonderful times. Not so long ago we were a very great power—perhaps the greatest—on the whole tundra."

"Yes, I'm sure that was so. But what happened to cause your change in fortune?"

"Ah, nothing happened all at once. We had some bad luck, that's all."

"Can you be more precise?" asked the Fox. "What was the first time you had bad luck?"

"Well," replied the Woolly Rhinoceros, "I suppose the first time was when we decided to put the Saber-Tooth Cats in their place."

"The Saber-Tooth Cats?"

"Yes, the Saber-Tooth Cats. They were jumping on everybody's backs and cutting them up with their fangs. So I decided that the peaceloving animals had to teach them a lesson."

"Did you?"

"Certainly. We attacked them and killed some of them."

"And your own herd, what happened to them?"

"Why is that important?"

"Please," said the Fox. "You were responsible for earthshaking events. We will all be in your debt if you reveal everything that took place."

"All right," said the Woolly Rhinoceros, who was pleased that his weighty historical role was finally being recognized. "The Saber-Tooth Cats ambushed us. They hid in the trees and leapt down on our backs. It was just bad luck that we happened to run under those trees. That's how the Cats managed to kill quite a few Rhinoceroses."

"I see. That must have been a serious loss. I suppose you were somewhat cautious after that—at least until you could regain your strength?"

"Cautious? Absolutely not! That's the way the weak animals behave."

"So what happened next?"

"I became aware that many of the other animals on the tundra, like the Musk Oxen, were saying that we had suffered a great defeat. It was even being put about that we were finished as a great power. So I knew what we had to do. We had to have a victory. I ordered an attack on the Woolly Mammoths."

"Why the Woolly Mammoths?"

"They were lording it over everyone. They thought their size gave them special privileges. I knew that if we defeated them everyone would have great respect for us."

"And how did that come out?"

"We gored quite a few Mammoths."

"But who suffered greater losses?"

"Unfortunately, we did. It was just our bad luck that their tusks were much longer than our horns. So right after that I launched the next campaign."

"The next campaign?"

"Yes, of course. If I didn't do something dramatic to reverse our fortunes, we would have lost everyone's respect."

"I see," said the Fox.

"So I decided the tundra would be better off without the Dire-Wolves. Those huge wild dogs were making everybody's life miserable."

"What was your plan?"

"We chased them. We were going to corner them and then stick them with our horns. But we had some bad luck. They led us into the tar pits. They were lucky. They were light and didn't sink in. But many Rhinoceroses did, and then the Dire-Wolves showed their true character. They acted like savage beasts. A few of us managed to escape."

"That's a terrible story," said the Fox sympathetically. "I suppose that you took special precautions after that to avoid danger?"

"When you've had a slight setback," answered the Woolly Rhinoceros, "you don't run and hide. I knew that now more than ever it was vital for us to show what we were made of."

"And how did you do that?"

"We launched a campaign against the Human Beings. They were getting too big for their animal skins."

"That was quite ambitious, wasn't it?"

"We needed a big success."

"Yes, of course. So how did you fare?"

"Unfortunately the humans surprised us. Instead of fleeing, they stood their ground. They set the end of their clubs on fire, and then they chased us."

"But they couldn't have chased you forever."

"No, they didn't. They came at us from all sides except one. Naturally we had to escape their fires, and there was only one way to go. It was just our bad luck that the only place to run was over a cliff."

"And you?" asked the Fox.

"Two of us escaped. We landed in a tree. But my friend, the other Rhinoceros, never recovered from two twisted ankles. He died two years ago."

"So you really are the last Woolly Rhinoceros on earth?" asked the Fox.

"Yes, that is so."

The two animals had been talking for a long time. The sun had passed overhead and was once again just above the horizon casting long dark shadows across the icy tundra.

The Fox knew that the most important part of the interview was still ahead. It would not be much of a history unless he was able to elicit the Woolly Rhinoceros's frank assessment of why these events had occurred. The Fox realized that he was taking on a tricky task. Would he really be able to get such a touchy beast to bare his chest?

After a pause the Fox resumed the conversation. "A remarkable story! Truly remakable!" The Rhinoceros's eyes lit up at these words which sounded like praise. "It would be so helpful," continued the Fox, "for the other animals on the tundra to hear what lessons you've learned from this history." The Rhinoceros's eyes clouded over with suspicion.

"Are you stirring up that ridiculous controversy all over again," asked the Rhinoceros, "about whether I made mistakes?"

"No. Certainly not," said the Fox, sensing that he might be on thin ice. "But you say there was a controversy. Did anyone have the. . .the gall to charge that your policy was a mistake?"

"Yes," answered the Rhinoceros, "that's generally known. There was some grumbling. But the fact is I had perfectly good policies. They were policies designed to restore the stature and pride of the Woolly Rhinoceros race. What can be wrong with that? They were policies intended to punish savages like the Saber-Tooth Cats and the Dire-Wolves. Who can find fault with an objective like that? We just had a little bad luck, as I've explained."

"I'm sure you're right," commented the Fox smoothly. "But if

I may just pursue this point a little further. . ." The Woolly Rhinoceros scowled and slowly lowered his head so that his long horn was pointing menacingly at the Fox. "Well," said the Fox hastily, "just so the world may understand fully the soundness of your decisions."

"All right. Proceed!"

"It would be interesting, and really quite instructive, to know how you handled this 'grumbling' of which you speak."

"Well, you may be sure I never admitted making mistakes—because, I didn't make any. But it was after the Dire-Wolves led us into the tar pits that a few of my assistants lost their nerve. They were afraid that the surviving Rhinoceroses were so dissatisfied that we might be overthrown. They said everyone would feel better—can you believe it?—that everyone would feel better—hah! hah!—if I admitted that I had adopted mistaken policies and then apologized." The Woolly Rhinceros was breathing hard. "Do you know what I told my assistants?"

"No. What did you tell them?"

"I asked them why leaders are chosen in the first place. To make mistakes? Of course not. They're chosen for exactly the opposite reason—because their followers think they won't make mistakes. So once a leader says, 'I'm terribly sorry, but I just made a mistake,' do you know what happens?"

The Fox said nothing. And then the Rhinoceros, acting out his answer, tilted his head over to the side, let his tongue dangle out, and twisted his eyeballs way up into his skull. "My assistants saw the implications pretty quickly," said the Woolly Rhinoceros a moment later.

The Fox was beginning to be a little disturbed at the direction the interview was taking. He had hoped to elicit comments about the true causes and the deeper significance of the Woolly Rhinoceros's experiences. Instead, he was getting a harangue about not admitting mistakes.

"Your analysis is very cogent," said the Fox. "But I'd like to ask you one more thing. You've said that you had a lot of bad luck. And, of course," added the Fox quickly, "you certainly did. But is it really possible that such a great animal as the Woolly Rhinoceros can be brought down just by bad luck? You are so powerful—what can it matter if you have some bad luck? Have you ever wondered whether there were other reasons for your misfortunes?"

The Woolly Rhinoceros stared hard at the Fox, and the Fox wondered if he would have to run for his life. But he stared back. Finally the Rhinceros let out a deep breath and spoke.

"I must admit," he said, "that you have been friendly. I think that with you I can reveal my true thoughts. Yes, I have wondered many times about just these questions as I've grazed by myself on the tundra." There was a silence.

"You know," continued the Woolly Rhinoceros, "I keep up a tough front. It's what I'm used to doing. And it's expected of me. But don't be deceived by appearances. I may look rough and tough, but don't assume that I don't think. When I think hard—and I've had lots of time for that lately—I can figure things out as well as the next animal."

"Never, not for a moment, did I assume that you don't think," interjected the Fox.

"So," said the Woolly Rhinoceros, "this is what I've figured out. The really big problems come when you start going downhill. Now maybe we should never have attacked the Saber-Tooth Cats in the first place. But it seemed a good idea at the time. Anyway, once that went badly, I was really in trouble."

"Why was that?"

"Well, once something's gone wrong, you have a hard choice. You can do nothing. But that means everyone sees that you're slipping. So you feel a big urge—really big—to do something. It's automatic, the way night follows day."

"Is there no way to get around it?" asked the Fox.

"I don't know. Maybe there is—if you're really number one and if no one can question that. Maybe if the Mammoths had some setback they wouldn't feel they had to do something to make up for it. After all, everyone knows they're on top. Now, to tell the truth, I was eager to prove the greatness of the Woolly Rhinoceroses.

"So," continued the Rhinoceros, "once you know you have to do something, the question becomes what. If you do something easy and safe like gouging a few sheep, what good will that do? You'll just be laughed at. That won't get you any respect."

"So you had to do something more ambitious?" said the Fox.

"That's right. Something really impressive."

"And that meant big risks, didn't it?" added the Fox.

"Obviously," agreed the Rhinoceros. "But then I told myself that great animals should be willing to take risks. And I always chose campaigns that I thought would be popular—like going after the Dire-Wolves and the Humans."

"Yes. No one likes them," said the Fox. "So you had the very best purposes. That is clear. But is that enough?"

For a moment the Rhinoceros seemed reluctant to speak. Then he said firmly, "No. It is not."

"And what can you say about the significance of what has happened?" asked the Fox. Again there was a long silence.

"It has been very difficult for me," began the Rhinoceros. "All those Rhinoceroses were my friends. You cannot believe—can you?—that I enjoyed seeing them stabbed to death by the Saber-Tooth Cats. Or that I liked watching them being eaten alive by the Dire-Wolves as they sank in the tar pits."

"But what did you think at the time?"

"I told myself and those who were left that if you really believe in the greatness of the Woolly Rhinoceros then there are some things worth giving up your Rhinoceros existence for."

"Well," said the Fox, "that could be true, couldn't it?"

"Yes," answered the Rhinoceros, "but I'm not so sure anymore. Especially if, after it's all over, there is no one left to enjoy being a Rhinoceros."

"But you are left."

It was a long time before the Rhinoceros spoke. At last, staring straight ahead, he said, "Do you think that I don't know what it means to be the last Woolly Rhinoceros?"

The sun had long since sunk beneath the horizon. There was now just a strip of pale red separating the black of the sky and the black of the earth.

"Thank you for your help," said the Fox to the Woolly Rhinoceros. "You have contributed to the Oral History of the Ice Age in a unique way. I wish you all good fortune on the tundra and . . . and . . . " The Fox suddenly found himself wishing to express a warm sentiment toward this great beast who was so alone in the world. "And, in all truth, I am sorry things could not have turned out differently."

"I have never talked so frankly with anyone," said the Woolly Rhinoceros. "I must admit that this thing you call—what is it?—Oral History?—may not be such a bad thing."

The Fox began to make his way back to his den. It would be some time before he could sort out the full significance of all that he had heard. The story of the Woolly Rhinoceros was indeed very strange. Perhaps even unique. Or was it?

THE PRACTICE
AND MALPRACTICE
OF DIPLOMACY

The Howler Monkey
Who Practiced Public Diplomacy

A LONG TIME AGO when human beings were experimenting with
the various means by which they might regulate their affairs and
bring about perpetual peace, a number of chieftains decided to
establish an assembly, or League of Tribes, in which they would
conduct public diplomacy and practice conflict resolution. In those
far-off times, as today, rumor spread quickly, and so when the
news reached the jungle, a Howler Monkey said to himself, "I

have something to contribute to this enterprise. I had better make my services available."

After a long journey to the coast, where the League of Tribes was situated, the Howler Monkey presented himself to a distinguished human being, who happened to be the Leading Chieftain.

"I am a specialist in communications," the Howler Monkey said to the Leading Chieftain. "I am here to offer my talents. You will do well to include me in your delegation to the League of Tribes."

The Leading Chieftain was not a little astonished by the cheekiness of this strange monkey. Why, he thought, should a mere monkey assume that he could teach something to humans about the art of communication? Nevertheless, he asked the Howler Monkey to explain himself.

Without further ado the Howler Monkey hunched his heavy shoulders, fixed a scowl on his face, opened his mouth wide and issued one of his remarkable roars. From inside the Howler Monkey there rose and spread out over everyone and everything a steady crescendo of thunderous rumbling sound. The trees shook and coconuts dropped. Minutes later, when the echoes were still ringing in everyone's ears, several of the Chieftain's ministers were found flat on their back, having been bashed on the head by falling coconuts, and others were staggering about in a daze.

The Chieftain knew instantly that a phenomenal resource had come his way. "Yes, you will be on our delegation to the League of Tribes," he announced to the Howler Monkey. "Now, let us discuss conference tactics. What will be the most advantageous moment for you to introduce your remarkable . . . uh . . . uh," the Chieftain groped for a word, ". . . utterance?"

"The moment the adversary begins to say something," responded the Howler Monkey.

"But how will we know what he's saying? You will drown him out," said the Chieftain.

"Exactly," replied the Howler Monkey. "If he thinks he's being listened to, he may get the mistaken notion that he has a logical case. And really, just between us, let's be frank. If you listen to him, there's always some risk that you'll think you see merit in what he says. And that, you must admit, would be a delusion. For, after all, is he not the adversary?"

"Yes, you certainly have a point there," said the Chieftain. "And are there any other times when you should deliver yourself of your . . . uh . . . utterance?"

"Certainly," declared the Howler Monkey. "Whenever you need to reply to the adversary and you have nothing sensible to say."

"But what good will that do?" asked the Chieftain. "If we don't have a good answer, why don't we just keep quiet?"

"You forget," replied the Howler Monkey, "there's a very simple law that it took me many years to learn: Weak Point Shout."

The League of Tribes opened amidst high optimism. The many chieftains took their assigned places in a beautiful grove of mango trees. A few keen diplomatic observers noticed that there was a large big bellied monkey, with a floppy throat sac, sitting with the humans in the front row of one of the delegations. It seemed a little strange, but no irregularity could be established since the monkey's papers of accreditation had been duly approved by the Credentials Committee.

A lesser chieftain, who was elected President of the League, welcomed all delegations to the historic opening seesion and then gave the floor to the Adversary Chieftain. As this important personage began to speak, there emanated from the Leading Chieftain's delegation—more precisely from the distended throat sac of the Howler Monkey—a vast rumbling roar which grew and swelled until it consumed everything and pressed up against all the chieftains and their advisers. A few minutes into the roar, the trees began to shake, and ripe mangoes splashed down on the heads of the chieftains. Amidst the confusion, several of them, keeping in mind what was truly important, commented to their aides, "Thank goodness we rejected the idea of meeting in the coconut grove."

After the President of the League of Tribes managed to restore order, he again recognized the Adversary Chieftain. But once more the mango grove was blanketed by an earthshaking roar. More ripe fruit splattered over the chieftains, many of whom sought, in vain, to get the floor in order to introduce procedural motions.

Finally, through the mechanism of exchanging handwritten notes, a recess was called to permit the Leading Chieftain and the Adversary Chieftain to conduct private consultations with a view to resolving the procedural difficulties that had arisen.

Meeting at the edge of the mango grove, the two great chieftains accused each other of bad faith. The Adversary Chieftain declared that it was unheard of in civilized diplomatic gatherings to permit monkeys to bellow. He had planned to make an unprecedented offer of accommodation designed to promote peace and now the conference had been turned into a shambles. The Leading Chieftain retorted that any offer of accommodation by the Adversary Chieftain could only be a deception. His delegation would do everything within its power to prevent the other delegations from being misled.

The first session of the League of Tribes ended inauspiciously. But the two most important delegations had at least been able to talk with each other, however acrimoniously, in private consultations.

Overnight each chieftain held a strategy session with his own delegation to consider the implications of the day's unusual events. Similar conclusions were reached by all delegations. The whole night was then consumed by frantic activity behind the scenes so that in the morning, when the second session of the League of Tribes was convened, a Howler Monkey was present in each chieftain's delegation. It was a day of prodigious production of sound.

It soon became apparent to everyone that business of any sort could only be accomplished in private consultations. At these times the Howler Monkeys were permitted to rest. They needed to preserve their energy for public sessions.

After the League of Tribes had been meeting for several weeks, the fallen mangoes began to ferment. They were put to good use. Following each session, the delegations gave parties and became inebriated eating the ripe fruit. And thus began the important tradition of intense socializing at major diplomatic gatherings.

The League of Tribes carried out its activities for many years. Much later, when the definitive scholarly history of diplomacy came to be written, the League was credited with one not inconsiderable achievement. It established once and for all the guiding precedents for large conferences: lots of noise at public sessions, serious business in private consultations, and an inexhaustible flow of refreshments.

The Sloth Who Was
A Master Diplomat

IN THE JUNGLES of South America there lived a sloth who possessed unusual talents. Few other animals knew that this shaggy doglike creature, who spent most of his time hanging upside down from branches high up in a tree, was capable of remarkable feats of diplomatic conciliation.

But down in the jungle there was a giant boa constrictor, a very old and savvy snake, who did know of the special skills of the sloth. And that is why the boa turned to his old friend the sloth for help when a conflict occurred which was threatening to ruin the jungle for everyone.

A terrible feud had erupted between two gangs of peccaries. For reasons that none of the other animals could make out, these two gangs of ferocious pigs were constantly charging at each other, gouging one another with their tusks, and grunting and shrieking all the time. They made the ground, which was pretty soggy to begin with, a sea of mud.

The other animals took their complaints to the big boa because he was the strongest animal in that part of the jungle. A mouse related how his spouse had drowned in the mud without a trace. A frog declared that in the terrible din created by the peccaries no other frogs could hear his beautiful croaking. An ocelot said that most of the little animals he ate were being scared away by all the noise. And a hummingbird had one of the saddest tales of all. The peccaries, he said, gave off a tremendous aroma when they were excited, which was now all the time. This overwhelming stench made it impossible to enjoy the smell of all the beautiful jungle flowers.

The boa, who also had a sensitive nose, knew that something had to be done. But these peccaries were clearly engaged in an unusually fierce quarrel. Exceptional skills would be needed to handle this dispute. And that is why the boa climbed up a tall tree one day and asked the master diplomat of the jungle, the sloth, to resolve this tenacious feud of the peccaries.

Once the sloth had agreed to act as a mediator, the boa slid back down the tree and began his preparations. He ordered the two gangs of peccaries to assemble at either end of a clearing and to await the arrival of the mediator. The peccaries didn't like this much but it was best to take the big boa seriously. After all, with his massive coils he could put some fairly unpleasant pressures on anyone who made him angry.

For most of a day everyone waited impatiently as the sloth slowly descended to a branch which overlooked the clearing. From there, hanging upside down, he could conduct the proceedings. By this time a great crowd of animals had come out of the jungle to watch.

The sloth spoke in the following manner:

"The first . . ." and there was a long pause.

"Order . . ." and then the sloth stopped and slowly moved his head to one side.

"Of business . . ." and after a few minutes the sloth moved his head to the other side.

"Is . . ." and once again there was a long pause as the sloth took several deep breaths.

"To decide . . ." and now many minutes passed as the sloth slowly shifted his gaze from one side to the other.

"On seating."

The first day was thus consumed entirely by matters of protocol. Many of the peccaries were still fidgety but some were obviously impressed by the great seriousness with which all the other animals regarded the proceedings.

During the second day when arguments on the merits were about to start, the sloth announced that there would be a recess. The sloth slowly moved back up the tree and down an adjacent tree. Then at his favorite spot the sloth executed his weekly urination. Slowly, moving each arm and leg one at a time, and always hanging upside down, the master diplomat gradually ascended and then descended again to the branch from which he presided.

After this three hour break, the sloth announced:

"We now . . ." and he paused for several minutes.

"Begin . . ." and then the sloth turned his head very gradually from side to side.

"Exploration . . ." and once again he halted in his delivery.

"Of the issues," concluded the sloth in a relative burst of speed.

The spokesmen for the two gangs of peccaries then began to denounce each other although neither could remember precisely why the other was at fault. It had, after all, been a rather long time since these proceedings had begun. The sloth, nevertheless, insisted with great fairness and deliberateness that each side be fully heard.

At the end of the third day, most peccaries on both sides appeared to have lost interest in what the sloth was doing. Indeed, a female peccary in one gang was ostentatiously making eyes at one of the more rugged males in the other gang. A few of the younger peccaries were flirting with squeals and grunts. And a general increase in belches indicated a growing hunger. When the sloth finally announced his decision—that both sides were equally blameless—all the peccaries felt great satisfaction. Since their former quarrel was now a pretty hazy memory, they wandered off to find meals and engage in other peaceful pursuits.

The mediation was over and all the animals were delighted. They crowded around the sloth to congratulate him. The big boa declared to the sloth:

"My friend, you are truly the master diplomat of the jungle. Tell us, what is the secret of your success?"

"Well . . ." said the sloth after he had waited a suitably long time to speak.

"Time . . ." and now the sloth paused for many minutes.

"Is . . ." and then the sloth very slowly moved his head from one side to the other to gaze at his admirers.

"The great . . ." and once again there was a long pause of several minutes.

"Healer."

The Animals Of The Lagoon Who Tried To Reason With The Electric Eel

"WELL, I don't set much store by affability." The speaker was a thick Electric Eel with tiny unblinking eyes.

"To tell the truth, I don't either," said a Giant Toad. "But we're not asking that you be a jolly fellow."

"Then what do you want of me?" asked the Eel.

An Otter spoke up. "We're only asking that you ease up a bit. We know that you have to eat. Like the rest of us. But when you throw one of those big bolts in the river you don't just kill the fish you're going to eat. A lot of others get cooked too. And there are many of us who've had so many shocks because of your eating habits that we're nervous wrecks."

"Yes," chimed in a Big Shrimp. "We're only asking that you be a little more considerate."

"And what's that supposed to mean?" demanded the Electric Eel a bit truculently.

"Well," commented a Turtle who often felt a bolt of electricity surge unpleasantly between his plates, "you could try to be a little more selective. You could fire off your bolts when the river is not so crowded with other animals feeding."

The Electric Eel stared sullenly at the Turtle. Realizing that he might have gone a little too far, the Turtle hastened to offer another suggestion, "Or perhaps you could give us all a little warning. Why not fire off, say, two light little spurts, and then most of us will know we have a few seconds to move before the big one hits?"

The animals of the Amazonian Lagoon nervously awaited the reply of the Electric Eel. After a long spell of suffering they had decided to put their case to the Eel. They had even been a little encouraged when the Eel agreed to meet with them under the conditions of a truce. There would be no bolts while the diplomatic explorations proceeded. But now as they looked into the hard unblinking eyes of the Eel and felt a faint tingling in the water, their confidence was ebbing.

"Do you realize what you're asking me?" said the Eel. No one spoke. "You're saying that I should change the way I've done things all my life—the way my mother taught me—and her mother taught her before that. Ways that have worked just fine. That's asking an awful lot." No one had anything to say.

"Okay. What's in it for me?" continued the Eel. "Well, I'll tell you. Absolutely nothing! I get plenty to eat doing just what I've always done. And I can't say that it bothers me very much that some of you are shaken up a little when I prepare for my meal."

Trying to save the situation the Giant Toad intervened some-what impulsively. "But you will get deep satisfaction from knowing that you have done the right thing."

"Yes," added the Big Shrimp, "and you will have earned our good will."

"Please," interrupted the Eel, "I've heard enough! This meeting is over!"

The animals of the Lagoon fled as fast as their fins and flippers would take them. The Turtle, however, was a little slow. He felt a terrible jolt as he reached the shore, one of the worst of his entire life.

The Otter made it safely to his nest up on the bank where his spouse awaited him. He told her of their polite and reasonable representations and, dejectedly, reported on the complete failure of their mission.

"Well, don't feel so badly," said the Otter's spouse. "You know, here in the Lagoon there are some things that just aren't going to get solved by diplomacy."

The Parrot Who Knew
All The Axioms Of Statesmanship

AN UNUSUALLY bright parrot lived for many years in the home of a human being who was the foreign minister of a large nation. The parrot therefore picked up a great deal of learning about the skill known as diplomacy.

When the foreign minister died, the parrot decided to return home to the South American jungle. His kin, a band of parrots, had been engaged in a long struggle with a family of ocelots. These cats had decided to enrich their diet by eating birds as well as monkeys and sloths. They had taken to climbing high into the trees where they sneaked up on the parrots and snared them in their nests. In retaliation, the parrots would circle around over the heads of the ocelots shrieking furiously so the cats could never get any sleep. Since both sides found the situation unsatisfactory, negotiations had begun in order to find a *modus vivendi*.

For the parrots it seemed an act of providence when their prodigal son showed up. He had immediately impressed them with his vast knowledge of diplomacy. Indeed, he knew forty-five of the most important axioms of contemporary statesmanship. The parrots therefore appointed him Chief Adviser and they even permitted themselves to hope that peace was at hand.

However, the negotiations were then at a standstill. The proposals of each side had been rejected by the other. And just recently the ocelots had raided several parrot nests. The parrots therefore asked the new Chief Adviser, "How can we revive the talks? Should we submit a new negotiating initiative?"

After a moment of silence the Chief Adviser responded: "No negotiation under pressure—no negotiation under pressure— no negotiation under pressure."

The parrots understood immediately. They knew that they were genuinely dedicated to peace. They desired constructive negotiations. But the ocelots, by raiding parrot nests only the night before, had engaged in an intolerable form of pressure. As the Chief Adviser had shrewdly pointed out, negotiations must not proceed under such circumstances. Still, the parrots were not entirely free of apprehension. They put another question to the Chief Adviser: "What will happen if the negotiations collapse?"

The Chief Adviser responded forcefully: "Bear the consequences—bear the consequences—bear the consequences."

The parrots asked themselves who must bear the consequences. The answer was obvious—the ocelots, of course. They were responsible for the aggression against the parrots and for the impasse in the negotiations. Yes, they would have to bear the consequences. And so, heeding the wise words of their new Chief Adviser, the parrots did nothing.

As time passed, the ocelots continued to snatch parrots and the parrots intensified their shrieking at the ocelots. After a sleepless month, the ocelots were anxious to get the parrots out of their hair. So they decided to make an offer which they believed the parrots could not refuse. They made the following sweeping proposal: "We will leave you alone if you will leave us alone."

The parrots were perplexed. The offer seemed too good to be true. They turned to their Chief Adviser. "How should we respond? Should we accept the ocelot offer as a basis for negotiations?"

The Chief Adviser delivered himself of the following opinion: "Negotiate from strength—negotiate from strength—negotiate from strength."

The parrots pondered over these profound words. They certainly recognized that they were not as strong as the ocelots. No parrot could destroy an ocelot in head-to-head combat. Since the ocelots were stronger, they surely wouldn't offer benefits to animals who were weaker. The ocelot proposal must therefore be a trap. The parrots wouldn't be negotiating from strength if they took up the offer. They rejected it.

The parrots then asked their Chief Adviser: "What kind of counterproposal should we make?"

After a moment of silence the Chief Adviser burst forth: "Stand

firm—stand firm—send a message—send a message—no concessions—no concessions."

The parrots found this a rich source of guidance. Why not propose an agreement that would provide complete protection? Why
not insist on this as a matter of principle? And so the parrots put
forth the following demand: "Under the agreement, ocelots shall
never climb into trees."

The ocelots denounced the proposal as one-sided. They accused
the parrots of lacking seriousness. "Why," they asked indignantly,
"should we be prohibited from climbing trees if we want to eat a
monkey or a sloth? What business is that of the parrots?" They
were so enraged that they even passed up numerous monkey meals
in order to concentrate on parrots.

After several weeks of intensified attacks from the ocelots, the
parrots again sought advice from their Chief Adviser. "The talks
are going nowhere," they complained. "Should we modify our
proposal?"

The Chief Adviser responded as follows: "Ball in their court—
ball in their court—ball in their court."

The game of tennis was, not surprisingly, an activity with which
the parrots of the South American jungle were unfamiliar. "Ball
in their court? What do you mean?" asked the parrots.

"Ball in their court—ball in their court—ball in their court,"
repeated the Chief Adviser. He also did not comprehend the rules
of tennis. He simply knew all the axioms of statesmanship.

"Please! Tell us what we should do."

Fortunately the Chief Adviser's phenomenal retention of axioms
came to his rescue. He managed to recall another phrase: "Their
turn to move—their turn—their turn."

The meaning of this instruction was readily apparent to the
parrots. They had made the last offer. Why should they retract it
and issue a new one? It was up to the ocelots to make a counteroffer
and they hadn't done so. If the parrots made a new proposal now,
wouldn't they simply be negotiating with themselves? The Chief
Adviser had saved them from a fundamental error.

The negotiations soon collapsed. The ocelots ravaged the nests
of the parrots with greater savagery than ever. And the parrots,
for their part, continuously prevented the ocelots from sleeping
by shrieking near their heads.

The Chief Adviser was long remembered by the parrots as the skillful diplomat whose knowledge of statesmanship had saved them from being coerced into agreement.

The Giraffe And The Hippopotamus
Who Talked Past Each Other

A GIRAFFE and a hippopotamus who had long been adversaries were being urged by the tick-birds who lived on their backs to work out ways to get along in a more harmonious fashion. The two great beasts began their discussions by the side of a watering hole.

"I propose," said the giraffe, stretching himself up to his full height, "that all animals with large jaws and sharp teeth refrain from opening their mouths in the presence of others. This will be an excellent measure for building confidence."

The giraffe's words floated into the air above the hippopotamus's head. The giraffe was pleased with his proposal and chuckled quietly.

The hippopotamus then said, "I propose that we agree to a universal halt to all hostile kicking. Indeed, in the interests of peace I declare that I will not lash out at other animals with my legs."

The hippopotamus's words passed under the stomach of the giraffe. The hippopotamus was also pleased with what he had said and grunted in satisfaction.

After a short time the two animals began to get fidgety and impatient. The hippopotamus opened his huge jaws and took a

134

bite out of the giraffe's thigh. The giraffe swung his front leg with all his strength and kicked the hippopotamus in the stomach.

A tick-bird who had watched the incident from close by said to the other tick-birds, "These big guys have made a mess of it again. Lopsided proposals may make you feel good—but not for very long."

The Monkeys Who Negotiated
With Masks

ONCE UPON A TIME on an island in the Indian Ocean there lived two rival troops of monkeys who had fallen into the practice of conducting prolonged negotiations. The subject was their strategic military strength which for these monkeys consisted of stockpiles of coconuts. Many of the coconuts had been placed on palm trees that were bent over and rigged as catapults. The negotiations had been motivated originally by the fear that someday the palm trees might snap their coconut projectiles by accident and bring about a war that none of the monkeys had desired. Also, many monkeys had been resentful that so many good coconuts were tied up in useless military stockpiles.

The negotiations were distinguished by their complexity and subtlety. The monkeys, who were exceptionally clever, had learned how to make masks. In a great spurt of creativity they had then designed and produced many different types of masks that could be worn at the negotiations.

The negotiations had been under way for many years when a new leader came to power in one of the troops. This monkey's strong suit was common sense, not brilliance. He would therefore have to be given extensive briefings so that he could quickly master the intricacies of these demanding negotiations and make sound decisions for the meeting which was to be held in a few days—the four thousand and seventeenth session.

A monkey who had long experience as chief negotiator gave the briefing. "This over here is our Resolute-In-Maintaining-Strength mask." The leader tried on a mask from which fearsome fangs protruded. The nose on the mask had distended nostrils and the eyes were narrow slits. "Now, this one," continued the negotiator, "is our More-In-Sorrow-Than-In-Anger mask which we use at the next meeting after our adversary has made a particularly stupid proposal." The mask was dominated by huge teardrops covering the face. The negotiator showed the leader the Limits-To-Our-Patience mask, the Determination-To-Work-As-Long-As-It-Takes mask, the Deeds-Not-Words mask, and many others.

The leader interrupted, "But tell me, what kind of an agreement would we really like to achieve?"

The negotiator had anticipated that the leader might ask simplistic questions and was ready with a reassuring answer. "You may be confident, sir, that our system makes it easy for you to put off that sort of decision. You know how hard it would be to get all the monkeys in the troop to agree on just what we should accomplish. The beauty of negotiating with masks is that all you have to do is decide which mask we should wear."

The leader went on to another question. "How do we make progress during a meeting? Suppose the adversary says something surprising, and you, as chief representative, want to reply in a way that's not consistent with your mask. Isn't it a little awkward—the whole delegation scrambling to change masks in the middle of the meeting?"

"Well," answered the negotiator, "there's never a need to change masks. We know what the adversary will say as soon as he arrives with a particular mask. And, of course, we know what we're going to say. Besides, if we changed masks during the meeting, the negotiations could speed up so much that there'd be no telling what might happen."

To permit the next meeting to take place on schedule, the leader approved the negotiator's recommendations for that session. As authorized, all the members of the delegation wore the Astonishment-And-Indignation mask. It had enormous round eye holes, eyebrows at the top of the skull, and a gaping mouth. By coincidence, the adversary also wore an Astonishment-And-Indignation mask of similar design.

When the initial pleasantries between delegations had been concluded, the negotiator, speaking from behind his mask, recited his prepared statement. "We are astonished—and I must say—even indignant, that at our last meeting you presented to us a proposal containing absolutely nothing new."

Speaking from behind his mask, the chief representative of the adversary replied, "We are completely surprised that your side has nothing constructive to say about our new proposal."

The negotiator, in accordance with his scenario, then said, "We cannot help but be surprised that you should adopt a posture of surprise."

The chief representative of the adversary rejoined, "We are naturally surprised that you should claim to be surprised because we are surprised."

The exchange continued in this vein until both sides had lost track of the logic of what they were saying. At this point, the two chief representatives confirmed that the next meeting, the four thousand and eighteenth, would take place in one week. The four thousand and seventeeth meeting was adjourned and the monkeys all shook hands amiably.

The negotiator reported to the leader. He commented that, thanks to the leader's wisdom in approving a sound posture, everything had gone precisely as predicted.

"But you didn't talk at all about stockpiles of coconuts or the deteriorating stability of the palm trees," complained the leader. "I have an idea. Why don't you go to the next meeting without masks?"

The negotiator became agitated. "That would put us in . . . in . . ." he had not anticipated such a radical challenge, ". . . in a highly vulnerable position. Our adversaries would gain a unilateral advantage. They would learn our secrets—and our thinking."

"You mean our absence of thinking." The leader's growing disenchantment was becoming apparent. "And what would happen," continued the leader, "if the adversary didn't wear a mask?"

The negotiator felt he was on firmer ground. "It would be a trick. They'd be wearing masks with moving parts—in order to get us to take off our masks."

Later, by himself, the leader reflected on the future of the negotiations. Should he approve the recommendation that the delegation wear the Eager-To-Make-Progress mask at the next meeting? It portrayed a monkey with a large panting mouth and hooting lips curled outwards—a monkey obviously in the grips of an ardent desire. The leader had heard enough to know that if things continued in the present way his successor would be approving masks for the five thousandth and probably even the six thousandth meeting.

In all fairness, the leader recognized that there were benefits from the present system. It kept a lot of monkeys busy and out of trouble. And there were remarkable technological spin-offs. The monkeys had learned to count to unusually high numbers.

In the end, the leader decided on a break with tradition. He appointed a trusted emissary, a monkey not working for the negotiator, and dispatched him to invite the adversary's leader to a meeting at a remote site on the island. There, without masks, the two leaders would discuss each other's concerns and practical ways to ease the dangerous coconut confrontation. The proposal was accepted.

When the two leaders met it did not take them long to recognize that someday the tautly stretched palm trees might accidentally snap and hurl coconuts at the adversary for no good reason. They therefore decided that they would no longer keep the trees loaded for instantaneous attack. They also adopted a procedure for gradually reducing the stockpile of coconut projectiles which would benefit both sides. The monkeys would eat them.

The two monkey leaders congratulated themselves. They agreed that there's just no substitute for the chief taking personal charge of a great enterprise.

DOCTRINES
AND
ILLUSIONS

The Wild Asses Who Believed In Their Own Virtue

HIGH ON THE Tibetan plateau there once lived a herd of wild asses who were convinced of their own virtue. Indeed, these asses enjoyed a privileged existence. There were vast spaces to run around in, endless fields of grass to chew on, pools of delicious melting snow to drink, and everywhere pure cold air to pull into their lungs. Over time the asses came to believe that it was no accident that they enjoyed these benefits. They must have deserved them—because of their superior virtue.

The leader of the herd was a magnificent ass. He had a golden coat of hair, huge thighs for running and jumping, and a massive head which he frequently held high, especially as he gazed at the snow-covered peaks on the horizon.

One day the leader addressed the herd. "It is our duty," he declared, "to strive with all our might to eradicate evil from this beautiful place. We know who are the cruelest animals on this plateau. I speak, of course, of the wolves." Whenever he referred to the wolves, the leader distended his sinewy nostrils in an expression of intense moral indignation.

"I call upon you," continued the leader, "to join me in a great crusade—to eliminate the wolves." Almost all the asses were deeply stirred and were ready to follow their leader. But there was one ass, deficient in fervor, who chose to question the leader.

"Why," he asked, "should we launch a dangerous campaign against the wolves? The sheep and the goats are their main victims. Besides, we can run faster than the wolves. The only way they ever get to kill one of us is if we're stupid enough to wander into deep snow."

The leader responded with eloquence. "We must be guided by principle. Whether the wolves kill few or many of us, they are in the wrong and we are in the right. We must be unyielding in our determination to fight evil." The leader was adept at inspiring his followers. Most of the asses were grunting and stomping in approval.

"But wait," insisted the ass who was afflicted with an excess of caution. "We don't have the power to defeat the wolves, much less eliminate them. What are we going to do?"

"I have a realistic plan," the leader answered. "The wolves are smaller than we are and our herd is bigger than their pack. We will charge at them, and with our greater speed and strength we will run them down, bite them, and kick them to death. The wolves have never been treated like that before. We will take them by surprise."

The leader lifted his head and gazed at the great snow-covered peaks towering above the plateau. "My friends, this is big sky country. It is not a land for timid asses. Never forget," he concluded, "when you have right on your side, there are no limits to what you can accomplish. For us, this campaign will be a test—a supreme test of our virtue and superiority."

The braying in approval of the leader was deafening. The issue was decided.

The wild asses launched their campaign against the wolves in high spirits. With the leader in front, they formed long columns and galloped off across the meadows. After several days they approached a pack of wolves feeding on a goat near the edge of the plateau. They charged full tilt at the wolves. As the leader had predicted, the wolves were completely surprised by this unorthodox behavior. The asses managed to kick several wolves to death and mortally wound a few others with their large teeth. But about half escaped.

That night the asses heard the howling of the wolves. "Listen to that!" cried the leader of the wild asses jubilantly. "We've frightened them badly. Tomorrow we'll press on with the attack."

Several days later, in ever higher country, the asses again met up with the wolves. This time the wolves fled upon sight of the charging asses. No wolves were caught. They led the asses high up onto the snow.

The asses were beginning to tire from the long charges. The days were getting shorter as winter approached and the nights longer and colder. When the asses next encountered the pack of wolves near the head of a steep valley, things turned out badly for the asses. They were hampered by the deepening snow. They were exhausted. Only one wolf was injured and several asses were killed.

During the night, the howling of the wolves reverberated back and forth between the mountain cliffs. It sounded as if there were a chorus of hundreds of wolves. Among the wild asses there was no jubilation. Many were eager to return to the safety of the plateau. Some were even beginning to question whether the whole campaign had been a mistake. During that cold, windy, black night the spirits of the asses sank to their lowest point.

The leader spoke to his followers. "Yes, the last few days have been trying. But we have finally cornered the wolves and they have no place left to run. We are close to success. Let us never forget—we are being tested and it is not in the nature of asses to give up in pursuit of a noble cause." The morale of the asses lifted and they gave their leader a vote of confidence.

On the next day, the asses struggled higher and higher following the trail of the wolves. The snow got deeper and deeper. By late afternoon the asses could barely move through the drifts. As darkness settled in, a blizzard began to rage. The asses were immobilized. They could not move forward or backward.

By morning all of the wild asses had frozen solid, just as they stood when the blizzard struck. Many months later when the snow began to melt, hundreds of asses were found high up in the mountains—rigid and upright.

The Gorilla Who Instructed
The Scholar

A HUMAN BEING who was one of that species' most distinguished students of power decided that his learning would never be complete until he observed directly how the *really* strong creatures of the earth managed their affairs. He therefore traveled to Africa and attached himself to a band of mountain gorillas that was led by a huge silverback male. This mighty gorilla was so powerful that he could put a log the size of a crocodile across his knees and snap it in two like a twig.

The ensuing days were arduous for the scholar. Running as fast as he could, constantly tripping over vines, he barely kept up as the gorilla band crashed through dense forests and charged up and down steep mountains looking for bamboo shoots to eat.

The scholar observed extraordinary events. He saw the gorilla leader in a fierce confrontation with another silverback. The two great apes stared at one another and strutted about stiffly. The hair on their heads stood erect. They beat their chests. And then they walked away in opposite directions.

One day the scholar saw a strange male gorilla approach the band, make eyes at one of the leader's females, take her by the hand, and run off with her. The leader appeared to notice the incident but did nothing at all about it.

On another occasion the scholar, crouching behind some bushes, watched with utmost fascination as a small male gorilla challenged the leader. The two gorillas ran about in circles kicking their legs violently into the air. They pulled up shrubs and flung them into the sky. They stuffed grass in their mouths and spat it out with great vigor. Then everything calmed down and everyone returned to feeding.

One night the renowned scholar of power built his nest of folded branches next to that of the great silverback. When they had both made themselves comfortable, the scholar spoke his mind. "I must say, my esteemed friend, I have studied your activities with bewilderment. You have such great power, but you never use it. You let everyone get away with murder."

The gorilla was surprised. What kind of strange primate was this that he had welcomed into his band? He decided, nevertheless, to speak politely. "What specifically have you found unsatisfactory?"

"Well," said the scholar, "you let that gorilla who was a complete stranger barge in and take one of your females. Wasn't that worth a fight?"

"Why?" the gorilla answered. "I had four females in the band. He didn't have any."

The scholar plunged on. "Several times you've been challenged by smaller gorillas. You could have torn them to pieces. Yet you always let them off without a scratch. I'll admit there was some pretty impressive chestbeating. But why didn't you follow through? Why did you always stop short of teaching them a real lesson?"

"Come to think of it," said the silverback, "we have a few gorillas in our band who go all the way when they attack. After they beat their chests, they rush at the enemy and bite him in the neck. But they're children. We punish them severely until they learn to control themselves."

The scholar would not give up. "But don't you care about your image? What about the perceptions of all your adversaries? What will happen when word gets around in the jungle that you make empty threats? Will you ever be safe again?"

The gorilla was very tired, but he decided he would try once more to make this peculiar primate understand. "Perceptions? Why should I worry about all that stuff? I've got a pretty good life here—lots of tender bamboo to eat, three charming wives, and a nice baby gorilla who plays on my stomach when I lie down at night.

"The main point," continued the gorilla, "is that I have a policy of avoiding violence. Why do you think I learned to beat my chest and do all those other crazy things? If I wound up fighting, that would be a complete failure of my policy. And why should I want to fail?"

The big silverback gorilla belched and went to sleep.

The distinguished scholar of power was deeply disappointed. He had come such a long way. He had exerted such great efforts. And he had learned so little.

The Imperial Mammoth Who Liked Things The Way They Were

IN THE ICE AGE an Imperial Mammoth came to the settled conviction that everything in life was just fine the way it was. With the self-assurance born of monumental size and the absence of challenge from anyone, he pronounced repeatedly to his friends, the Musk Oxen, the Rhinoceroses, the Bison, and the Horses, that any animals who tried to change things were nothing but troublemakers.

And so the Imperial Mammoth felt a keen sense of outrage when he saw that a herd of Giraffe-Camels had migrated into his territory and was consuming the grass and shrubs. Convinced that this was a challenge bringing into question his credibility with all the lesser animals, the Imperial Mammoth charged at the Giraffe-Camels. However, these lithe and leggy creatures easily evaded their ponderous attacker. And no matter how often he chased them the result was always the same.

Brimming over with indignation, the Imperial Mammoth became more determined than ever to teach a lesson to these upstarts. Failure was an unthinkable outcome. The Imperial Mammoth therefore lumbered after the Giraffe-Camels day after day and week after week. He was forced to snatch all his meals on the run, and he was even too exhausted to perform the stately maneuvers of sex.

And so the way of life of the Imperial Mammoth came to be changed entirely—as he persisted in a stupendous effort to preserve the status quo.

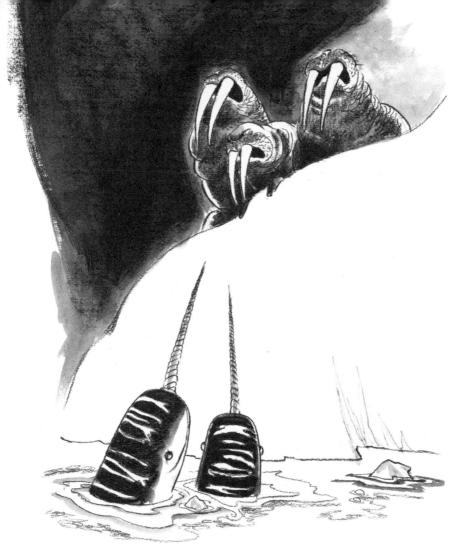

The Walrus Who Believed In
The Balance Of Power

THE LEADER of a herd of walruses set great store by the balance
of power. He was convinced that the greatest threats to peace
occurred whenever the balance was not satisfactory. The herd
therefore struggled unceasingly to improve the balance.

On one occasion the walruses encountered a herd of narwhal. The walrus chief decided that these sea mammals—the unicorns of the ocean—were potentially more powerful than the walruses. "Look," he said to his herd, "everyone of their warriors has a long tooth that sticks way out like a spear. You get stuck with one of those things and you're finished." And so, to preserve the balance of power, the walruses launched a surprise attack. They cut hundreds of narwhals to ribbons with their tusks.

Later the walruses ran into a school of beluga whales. The walrus chief judged that these small white whales and the walruses possessed roughly equal power. "This situation is highly dangerous," he told his followers. "It lends itself to miscalculation. What if the belugas think they are stronger than we are? Then there will be terrible trouble." And so, to ensure that the balance of power was not jeopardized by miscalculation, the walruses attacked the belugas. They impaled dozens of them.

After a while, the walruses found themselves in the vicinity of a small herd of seals. They outnumbered them two to one. And the seals had no tusks or weapons of any kind. "Look at those pitiful seals," said the walrus chief. "Their power is puny. They must be beside themselves with anxiety. They are probably plotting some last-ditch effort to shift power in their favor. This is exactly the type of imbalance which leads to instability." And so, to prevent the seals from taking a desperate and rash act designed to upset the balance of power, the walruses launched a massive attack. The seals were decimated.

When the engagement was over, the walrus chief declared to his herd, "We have done our duty. We have established the best possible balance of power—overwhelming superiority."

The Baboon Who Couldn't Tell Dreams From Reality

ONCE UPON A TIME there was a baboon chief who came to be deeply dissatisfied with the lot of the baboons. He was obsessed with the lack of respect accorded baboons compared, for example, with elephants, crocodiles, lions, or rhinos. Remembering what he had learned from his parents—that long ago baboons were twice their present size—the baboon chief fell to dreaming about a world in which baboons towered above the lion. Indeed, in these intensely vivid dreams leopards, lions, and even rhinos, scurried away abjectly whenever a big baboon approached.

Now his waking hours were nowhere near as pleasant. And so, determined to correct this unsatisfactory state of affairs, the baboon chief called together his troop and spoke to them with great sincerity. He told them that it was once again time for baboons to be respected by all the animals on the plain. They would be held in awe if, like their ancestors, they were simply twice as big. He enjoined them to display confidence and to be bold. "Above all," he concluded, "there is one thing every loyal baboon can do to restore the greatness of the baboon race. Let us all stand tall!"

The baboons responded enthusiastically. They were, after all, loyal baboons who respected their leader. And so the baboons were soon strutting around, holding themselves in an unnaturally upright position. They stumbled constantly, but most maintained a fixed and resolute smile. On one occasion a number of upright baboons teetered toward a few browsing rhinos. When the rhinos, shocked by these oddly shaped primates, lumbered off into the distance, the baboon chief was elated. Standing tall would transform baboon stature in every way.

Of course, the baboon chief did not stop dreaming of the times when his ancestors were twice as big. But now since both his sleeping and waking hours were equally delightful he began to get thoroughly confused. He could no longer distinguish reality from dreams. In fact, he had no inclination whatever to do so.

One day a number of unanticipated events occurred. A baboon who had been standing tall with utmost diligence fell to the ground moaning and clutching his back. He had been stricken by lower back pains. The new and unusual method of locomotion was taking its toll. Then another baboon collapsed, his smile transfigured into a hideous grimace. This poor animal was soon snatched by a leopard.

As more and more baboons were afflicted with excruciating back pains, the baboon chief became impatient. "You are imagining these complaints," he told his comrades. "They are nothing but dreams. Just concentrate—use your will power and they will go away."

But lower back pains did not go away. And soon the policy of standing tall came to be controversial. Some baboons, like the chief and his supporters, believed that standing tall was a patriotic duty even if spinal dislocation caused discomfort. Others said that the baboon chief was out of touch with reality and was destroying baboon society. Some of these baboons even ridiculed the dreams of their chief. "When baboons were twice their size," commented an erudite baboon, "there were also giant pigs, huge rhinos, and tremendous sheep. What was so special about us? The chief mis-remembers the past and misapplies it to the future."

Baboon society was deeply divided. The two factions hurled uglier and uglier accusations at each other—especially about who should be blamed for the growing number of successful attacks by lions and leopards. As more and more baboons were stricken, the ranks of the chief's opponents steadily grew.

For the baboon chief these were distressing times. The lions and the leopards were supposed to be their main enemies. Why should baboons within his own troop behave as if they were enemies too? Not surprisingly, the chief frequently took comfort in his nighttime visions, which more than ever seemed real to him. His daytime travails, however, were obviously nightmares. It was clear to him that he would have to get himself out of this bad dream. But how?

The solution turned out to be quite simple. The baboon chief decided that he did not wish any longer to be leader of a bunch of baboons who were continuously groaning about their lower back pains. He would refuse to be their leader.

The baboon chief's offer of resignation was readily accepted, a development which momentarily astonished him, until he remembered that curious things always happen in dreams. And so the baboon chief spent his remaining years happily transfixed by the reality of his fantasies—about the glorious times when all other animals stood in awe of big baboons.

The nightmare was over. For everyone.

The Butterflies Who Slew
The Dragon

ONCE UPON A TIME there was a swarm of butterflies who enjoyed an idyllic life on a beautiful patch of land alongside a river in Africa. Their irridescent purple and yellow wings flashed in the light as they fluttered among an abundance of flowers and feasted endlessly on nectar. Truly the sun shone on these privileged creatures.

Then one day a gang of crocodiles crawled out of the river and pushed and shoved their way onto this lovely spot of land. They crushed the flowers. They thrashed around chewing up other animals and splattered mud all over. The invasion of the crocodiles was a devastating event for the butterflies.

Most of the butterflies felt they had no choice but to find another home. However, one butterfly was incensed by the injustice of the invasion. "We were here first," he said. "We were doing no harm to anyone. We just wanted to be left alone."

"Those are fine sentiments," commented another butterfly, "but what can we do about it?"

"Well, we should drive the crocodiles off!"

Several butterflies tittered. "That's a good one! How can a few butterflies force the crocodiles to do anything? They are the mightiest creatures and we are the most delicate. Do you think that we should eat the crocodiles?" A few butterflies were so convulsed by tittering that they lost control and fell to the ground.

"We must exercise our brain power," answered the assertive butterfly, "and then we will be able to overcome this challenge."

The idea was a novel one. In their favored existence, the butterflies had gained little experience in overcoming challenges. And

157

in fact, so tiny were their brains that most of them were unaware that they had any.

Nevertheless the insistent butterfly, who appointed himself commander of all the butterflies, formed a committee and eventually a strategy was conceived. The butterflies would fly in a rush at the heads of the crocodiles. They would produce a sinister whirring of their wings. Then they would unfurl their long proboscises and stick the crocodiles in the eye.

Despite their flightiness, many of the butterflies took on a new seriousness of purpose. They trained intensively, rushing at each other, extending and retracting proboscises, beating their wings furiously, and thrusting forward antennas aggressively. It would have been hard for the dimmest of butterflies not to sense that a great enterprise was about to commence.

At last, one sunny day, the butterfly onslaught was launched. But things did not turn out as planned. Going into combat for the first time, many of the attackers felt very nervous. Their aim became unsteady. Their proboscises often missed crocodile eyeballs and rubbed instead against scaly eyebrows. Sore butterfly tongues were the main product of the first engagement. And worst of all, the crocodiles seemed to take no notice whatsoever of these arduous butterfly exertions.

But the butterflies persisted. They became not only more skillful, but much bolder. Hovering just above a crocodile eye, a combat-seasoned butterfly would wait until the lid was fully raised, and would then push, swirl and scrape its stiff proboscis all around the monster's eyeball until the mighty beast was forced to jerk his head away. These tactics were not, of course, without risk. Sometimes when a crocodile jerked his head and clamped his jaws shut, a brave butterfly would suddenly find himself ground to pieces.

In time the crocodiles were unable to ignore the implacable assault of the butterflies. In fact, butterfly proboscises came to be a torment. And so, one by one, the great crocodiles began to lumber off into the water to find more congenial surroundings.

The butterflies were elated by their victory. Few had ever imagined they would really succeed—that the lightest of creatures could impose their will on the most massive. But they knew they had been fighting a just war against an evil enemy. Indeed, they had slain the dragon.

A profound change occurred in butterfly character. No longer were they creatures dreaming only about where they would find their next sip of nectar. Now they were conscious that they had performed heroic deeds. They were liberators. They were creatures of superior virtue who could perceive injustice and who had the boldness to remedy it. The butterflies came to believe that these were the qualities which constituted their essential nature as butterflies.

And so it was not long after their remarkable military victory that the butterflies began to experience a deep sense of letdown. They longed for the days when their lives had been absorbed by a lofty sense of mission and bravery had been demanded of all of them. If their essential nature called for the righting of wrongs, how could they justify their existence doing nothing day after day other than enjoying the flowers?

When their spirits had sunk very low, the butterfly commander decided that it was imperative to launch a new initiative. "We cannot go on like this," he said to his fellow butterflies. "It is unnatural for butterflies to be so dejected. We must be true to our natures. We must fight evil wherever it exists. Let us find a new dragon to slay."

Butterfly scouts set out in all directions. Soon one of them found what they were after. A little way into the jungle stood an old tree with a gash in its bark. Sap oozed from the gash and attracted many insects. But as they arrived to feast on the sap the insects were ambushed by a band of wasps who stabbed them and shot them full of paralyzing venom.

A high degree of anticipation, even excitement, came over the butterflies when they heard about this insect holocaust. "These wasps are vicious," declared the butterfly commander. "They inflict excruciating pain and suffering. They are treacherous and terrorize everyone. They are absolutely evil." All the butterflies agreed.

"This is just the job for us," continued the butterfly commander. "We'll drive the wasps off—the same way we took care of the crocodiles."

"This will be much easier," said another butterfly. "The wasps are puny compared to the crocodiles."

Once again the butterflies prepared themselves for a great adventure. They trained intensively, flapping their wings with great vigor, unfurling their proboscises, and thrusting forward their antennas in a pugnacious fashion. Butterfly morale soared. They experienced a new buoyancy.

The butterflies launched their attack confident of quick victory. The first wave of butterflies rushed forward with their antennas pointing rudely at the wasps and their wings whirring with menace.

The wasps, for their part, were astonished. They did not take kindly to interference from outsiders. Being no-nonsense types, the wasps zoomed in on the butterflies, bit them in the head, and neatly sliced off their wings at the joints. They carried off the corpses to a nearby nest where they were stacked for later consumption.

A second wave of attacking butterflies met the same unpleasant end. Soon there was a growing pile of irridescent purple and yellow butterfly wings lying on the ground.

The butterfly commander could not escape the obvious conclusion. The butterflies were suffering a stinging defeat. The commander called off the attack.

After the surviving butterflies had returned to their home territory, the commander addressed his dejected comrades. "Let us always remember," he began, "that we were the ones who defeated the mightiest of beasts, the crocodiles. Today's unfortunate setback does not change a thing. As butterflies it is in our nature to be liberators and to do good. And we shall do so many times in the future. We will only need to do one thing differently." The butterfly commander paused.

"We just have to choose a little more carefully which dragons to slay."

MISTAKES BIG
AND
REALLY BIG

The Baboons Who Wanted To
Make The Leopards Impotent
And Obsolete

DEEP IN AFRICA a troop of baboons was engaged in a most unusual project. They were constructing a large net that would extend over the place where they lived—a rocky clearing in the forest.

The baboons had been inspired by their leader, who had shared with them a dream. He had told them that baboons—fathers, mothers, and baby baboons—should all be free from the threat of attack from leopards. "We are capable of great achievements. We are the smartest and most talented animals in the forest. I call upon you," the leader had concluded, "to build a shield over our homes that will make the leopard impotent and obsolete."

Accepting the challenge, a particularly brainy baboon had been appointed czar of the project. The czar had supervised months of research into all possible ways to construct nets over their homes. He and his associates had woven nets from rushes, but these were so dense that they would have condemned the baboons to live in darkness. Then they built a net of thin vines, but when the strands had dried out they became brittle and broke.

The baboon czar would not accept defeat. Achievement of a glorious goal was at stake. And so he eventually arrived at a new and ingenious solution. He found that there was one type of spider web which consisted of unusually strong strands. When these were braided together, they formed a tough and flexible fiber. The great construction effort then proceeded rapidly and a large white canopy soon extended over the rocky home of the baboons.

It was time to test the structure. Several enthusiastic baboons volunteered to leap from a nearby tree to see whether the net would hold. But the baboon czar saw immediately that none of these candidates was suitable. They were all young, lean, and athletic. None was as heavy as a full-grown leopard. And so the czar surveyed the troop and found an older male baboon, once a famous warrior, who had grown obese. The warrior was easily persuaded to make this dangerous leap into a net of uncertain strength, since he remained a staunch baboon patriot.

The czar then reported to the baboon leader: "It is essential that we conduct a test under the most realistic conditions that can be anticipated. I have arranged for the heaviest baboon in the troop to leap into the net." The leader was pleased, and the czar felt that praise for his efforts was fully justified. After all, not everyone would have been so clever as to calculate that the baboon who jumped into the net must weigh as much as a leopard.

On the day of the test the leader and all the other baboons turned out to watch. The old obese baboon hauled himself to the top of a nearby tree. The baboons of the troop, who normally chattered continuously, observed him in silence. The old baboon leaped into space. He landed in the middle of net. The net sagged—but held.

The baboons cheered wildly. And then the baboon leader spoke with considerable eloquence, extolling the dedication and skill of the baboon czar and his team. The leader had never doubted that baboons were capable of great feats of creativity.

Thereafter the baboons spent most of the time under their protective shield. They came to have complete confidence in it. Soon a profound change occurred. The baboon troop abandoned the requirement of sentry duty and all the other rigors of providing for their defense.

One day many months later a couple of leopards climbed into the tree which overlooked the home of the baboons. When they saw the large webbed canopy below them they were puzzled, never having seen anything like it before. But after a few minutes, one of the leopards said, "Even if we can't see them, I know there are a lot of baboons down there."

"We haven't eaten in days," said the other leopard. "Let's jump through that thing and get a good meal."

The two leopards then leaped out of the tree and soared toward the net. They landed together and the net collapsed. Underneath, the baboons were totally unprepared. Half a dozen baboons were torn to pieces within minutes. The slaughter was terrible.

The baboons who escaped, including the leader, were very angry. A court of inquiry was organized and the baboon czar was put on trial. In his defense he declared repeatedly:

"Nobody can think of everything."

The Octopus Who Was
In A Tight Spot

A MORAY EEL, peering out from his coral cave at the bottom of a tropical sea, spied a small octopus drifting toward the entrance to the cave. When the octopus got close, the eel darted out and clamped his jaw on one of the octopus's tentacles. The eel rotated his thick snakelike body round and round, twisting the tentacle tight.

"Ouch," said the octopus. "My tentacle is going to come off. Can't we negotiate a fair solution to this problem?"

The moray eel rotated again. "Yesh," he hissed through his gritted teeth, which were still fastened on the octopus. "I'm always prepared to negotiate a fair solution in mushual interesh of the parties."

"I propose," whispered the octopus, who was feeling faint from his discomfort, "that you let me go and then I'll fetch you a minnow to eat."

The moray eel twisted around sharply and snapped off the octopus's tentacle.

"What did you do that for?" asked the shocked octopus. "You promised to negotiate."

"Why should I waste time negotiating with someone who offers me a minnow in exchange for a whole octopus arm? Next time when the sishuashion is serious," said the eel as he munched his meal, "don't make a frivolous offer."

The Seals Who Vilified The Iguanas

A HERD OF SEALS lived on a remote island in the ocean. Nearby, on a rocky outcropping, a colony of large marine iguanas made its home.

The two groups disliked each other. The seals thought the iguanas were ugly and uncouth. Moreover, the iguanas practiced a different system for reproducing themselves. They laid eggs. The seals found this incomprehensible and repugnant.

The iguanas, for their part, resented the easy lifestyle of the seals who glided effortlessly through the water. The iguanas felt the seals were show-offs.

But neither group saw it in its interest to start a fight with the other. The teeth of the seals were not long enough to pierce the scaly hide of the iguanas. And the iguanas, being vegetarians, could not eat the seals.

Within the seal colony, feelings against the iguanas often ran quite high, especially whenever seals were competing for leadership. An old bull seal who wished to retain his position as chief decided that he would please his herd by launching a propaganda compaign against the iguanas.

Soon a choir of seals began bellowing across the waves:

"See what heavy scales the iguanas have. What do they need so much armor for? For self-defense? Don't delude yourselves. They must be planning aggression. No birds or fish are safe. The iguanas may devour you at any time."

The iguanas were shocked when they heard these malicious accusations. After all, they were vegetarians.

A sagacious old iguana advised the chief of the iguanas, "The seals know that we eat only seaweed. They know we never attack fish or birds. Why would they accuse us of preparing to commit an aggression which we are incapable of? Obviously, the seals are justifying in advance an aggression they intend to commit against us."

"Right now," continued the iguana adviser, "we are very weak. Our teeth and jaws are capable of masticating only seaweed. In view of the imminent aggression of the seals, our only course is to launch a program to learn to eat fish, birds—and seals."

The iguana chief approved this recommendation. All iguanas were ordered to desist from eating seaweed and to begin devouring fish and birds. For many, chewing on flesh was at first highly distasteful. But most got used to it. Moreover, teeth got sharper and jaws stronger. And many iguanas grew into fierce hunters.

When the leader of the seals learned of these developments, he delivered a somber message to his herd. "Our worst fears about the iguanas have been realized. They are chewing up thousands of innocent creatures all over the ocean. We must institute military training for our young bulls so they can defend us against the aggressor."

And thus began the era of prolonged hostility between the herd of seals and the colony of iguanas.

The Two Pieces Of Elbow Bone That Had Much In Common

ONCE UPON A TIME, many millions of years in the future, strange creatures came to Earth from a faraway place and, after rummaging around a bit, found two tiny pieces of bone. They took these back with them and put them in a display case for the edification of the other strange creatures with whom they lived.

After a while, one of the two pieces of bone, which were lying side by side in the display case, decided to make the acquaintance of the other.

"How do you do," said one of the tiny fragments. "I was once part of an elbow. May I inquire to whom or to what you once belonged?"

"What a coincidence!" replied the other fragment. "I, too, was part of an elbow."

"I see. And in what kind of creature?"

"In a monkey."

"Well, I was in an elbow of a very important creature, a human being—someone called 'The President.' Tell me, what was it like to be part of an elbow in a monkey? What were your happiest moments?"

"I was most content," said the monkey elbow fragment, "when I could help my owner be happy. She was a lovely lady monkey. I made it possible for her to extend her arm and touch all her friends. And what about you? What were the happiest moments in your life?"

"I also sought to please my master," said the other elbow fragment. "The President got the most satisfaction out of using his right arm for sports. I was a very hard piece of elbow. The President could always count on me when he put his arm on the table and arm-wrestled with other human beings."

"That must have been fun!"

"Yes, it was," declared the elbow bone of the President. "But didn't you ever do something more important than help the lady monkey touch other monkeys? Something more . . . more lasting . . . more historic?"

After a pause the piece of monkey elbow replied. "Yes, I did. I also was part of a right arm. My goodness! We do seem to have so much in common. Well, being an elbow, I helped my mistress to lift babies to her breast. But you must have done important things, too."

"I certainly did. I remember once I helped the President to lift his arm to the table. Then he reached for a pen and he wrote some words on a paper. He was very satisfied. He kept saying, 'Just what we need . . . just what we need . . . an ultimatum . . . that's the only language they understand . . . that will convince them of our resolve . . . now there will be peace . . . peace with honor.' I knew," continued the fragment of the President's elbow, "that we had done something really important. I could feel it in my entire bone."

"And what happened then?"

"Nothing much at all. I just kept on being part of the President's elbow bone. Of course, that was close to the time when everything changed."

"Changed? In what way?"

"That was about the time the President disappeared, and all his bones, except for this piece of elbow bone, which is me."

"I'm just amazed! We do have so much in common, " said the piece of monkey bone. "That's exactly what happened to me, too. The lovely lady monkey disappeared, and every other part of her except this little piece of bone, which is me."

The Animals Of The Farm
Who Were Attacked By The Bees

ONE WARM SUMMER DAY, the animals on the farm witnessed an extraordinary event. From out of the beehive zoomed a large bee. It picked up more and more speed as it flew in tighter and tighter circles. Finally, with a high-pitched whining sound filling the air, the bee rocketed with incredible velocity into the side of a horse. The horse staggered and collapsed. As the horse shuddered in its final spasm, no one could tell if its death had come from acute shock, or venom, or both.

The peaceful animals of the farm were aghast. The bees had always been something of a nuisance, but nothing like this had ever seemed possible. The cows were particularly shaken by the tragedy. They feared that the bees had developed a frightful new method of attack. A pigeon who had witnessed the event from a nearby fence confirmed that the bee had adopted an entirely new aerodynamic pattern. A pig, realizing that if a horse could be felled so could he, warned that absolutely nobody was safe anymore. He was confident that the bees intended to kill or coerce all the rest of the animals.

Then another frightful event took place. Again a bee shot out from the hive, spiralled around furiously, and this time slammed into the side of an ox. Once again the stricken animal collapsed, shuddered and died.

The animals of the farm were now convinced that the bees had taken a decision to increase vastly their ability to strike down anyone and everyone. A chicken asserted that the bees must be intent on a campaign of terror and intimidation. Clearly, the bees had decided to try to take over the farm. Any other explanation, agreed a rooster, would be self-delusion.

Only an owl raised questions. What was the evidence that the bees had adopted a sinister plan? True, the recent events had been shocking. But could they be a result of some aberration rather than a grand design? And what could the farm animals do as a practical matter to protect themselves? The owl counseled against reaching hasty judgments. Before they launched elaborate schemes to counter the bees, they should learn more about why the tragedies had occurred.

The other animals were impatient with the owl's caution. Some, in a very impolite fashion, mocked him by hooting him down. A chicken even questioned his loyalty. She suggested that the owl had secret sympathies with the bees. After all, didn't the owl also engage in surprise attacks against his victims? The owl was driven out of the barn.

And so the animals proceeded to take special measures to protect themselves. A patrol of dogs was organized to keep constant watch on the beehive and to bark a warning if any bees exited with unusual velocity. The larger animals scraped away laboriously digging holes into which everyone could dive in the event of an alarm. Evacuation exercises were conducted.

In short, the animals abandoned their prior way of life. They devoted themselves entirely to defense. Discipline, drill, and dedication soon dominated their existence. Gaiety, whimsy, and charm were things of the past.

No new attack took place for many months. A clever crow explained that the bees had evidently completed their program of testing without any hitches. This indicated an unusually successful development effort by the bees. The animals would be vulnerable to a surprise attack if they let down their guard. Tension remained high. The animals continued their patrol and defense drills.

Many years later, an ant who had been trained as a spy managed to crawl into the beehive and to return safely. The ant had found no unusual activity in the hive. He had overheard, however, a number of bees reminiscing about the terrible summer in which two bees had gone berserk after making honey from contaminated pollen.

HYPOCRITES—
GENIUSES—
AND OTHER
DANGEROUS TYPES

The Pig Who Abhorred Injustice

IN THE FOREST of South America there once lived a herd of wild pigs whose members were frequently victimized by ferocious predators. The pigs were always on the run. As they fled from danger to danger they were barely able to snatch enough nourishment to stay alive—a few roots and nuts. For most of the terrified and emaciated pigs life was hardly worth living.

The leader of the herd was a pig who happened to be possessed of lofty sentiments and great eloquence. When a sow was overrun by a horde of army ants and torn into a million little pieces, the leader stood over the bones and orated thusly: "I abhor injustice. This beautiful sow was a threat to no one. Why cannot all creatures live in peace?"

When a piglet was crushed in the coils of an anaconda and then swallowed whole, the leader declared with fervor: "I detest violence. Every life is sacred. Let us all love each other."

When an old boar was carried off in the teeth of a jaguar, the leader proclaimed: "The powerful must never terrorize those who are old or weak. We must all strive for peace and justice."

After many years of such events, the leader happened to take his herd to a plateau where, by good luck, there were no army ants, no giant snakes, and no jaguars. Suddenly the pigs were able to feed at their leisure on small animals who lived in the grass. In no time at all, the pigs transformed themselves from weak and fearful creatures into strong and assertive beasts.

The leader of the pigs was able to deliver his orations in firmer and more ringing tones than ever before. After he had gobbled up a frog, he declared: "This frog has committed aggression against innocent grasshoppers. And I abhor aggression."

When he had crunched through the shell of a mud turtle, he proclaimed: "Turtles terrorize the small and the weak. They murder many, many minnows. We must all condemn such terrible injustice."

And after he had finished munching on a mouse, he delivered himself of these words: "This mouse has heartlessly ended the lives of countless worms. Indeed, he has waged a war on worms. I abhor every form of injustice."

In time, there was scarcely a living thing that survived the pig leader's abhorrence of injustice.

The Lizard Who Played Fast And Loose With His Tail

ONE DAY in the desert a lizard was about to devour a delicious meal—an egg that had been laid by a hawk—when suddenly above the lizard there was a whoosh of air and the beating of wings. A very angry mother hawk was swooping down towards the lizard. With not a second to spare the lizard shook his tail violently, the tail broke off and began to squirm convulsively in the dust, and the hawk's talons seized the twitching tail while the lizard sprinted to safety.

Now this lizard happened to be remarkably proficient at throwing his tail. In fact, eighty-seven times he had gotten into life-threatening situations. Eighty-seven times he had confused his attacker by throwing off his tail. Eighty-seven times he had saved himself from destruction. And eighty-seven times he had grown a new tail.

The eighty-eighth tail, however, was no ordinary tail. He was uncommonly perceptive. He knew that he was much younger than the lizard and he began to wonder what had happened to all the previous tails. He decided that he'd better have a serious talk with the lizard.

"You know," said the tail to the lizard, "I am vital for your survival."

"Yes, of course," answered the lizard. "You certainly don't need to remind me of that."

"If you get into trouble and throw me to the rear, it's the end for me. I'll just twist and squirm for a few seconds—and then I'm done for. Finished for good. It's not a satisfying way to end one's days."

"I understand fully," said the lizard soothingly.

"So I'd like to have some assurances. I'd like to know that I'm not going to be sacrificed for a trivial reason. There needs to be some trust between us."

"Tell me. How can I put your fears to rest?"

"Well," said the lizard's tail, "I'd like to be sure that you won't be reckless, that you won't take unnecessary risks."

"Never fear," said the lizard. "There is not a more prudent reptile in the whole desert than myself."

"And I would like to be consulted if a dangerous situation is about to arise and it becomes unavoidable that the two of us must face some great peril."

"You have my word," said the lizard, "we will consult fully— and in advance—if peril should ever be imminent."

"Thank you," said the tail. "I am most appreciative."

Several days later, during his perambulations across the desert floor, the lizard remembered that he had recently seen some empty rattlesnake eggshells nearby. "Hmm," he said to himself, "there must be a few tender baby snakes over there that will make a tasty meal—providing I can dart in and out before their mother sees what I'm doing."

The lizard said nothing about these plans to his tail. He simply scuttled off in quick spurts toward the mound of stones where the rattlesnakes made their home. When the lizard's tail began to suspect that their journey was not aimless, the tail said to the lizard, "Where are we going?"

"Nowhere special," answered the lizard. "I am just strolling."

When the lizard got to the rattlesnake den, he found himself facing not a few helpless babies but a large angry hissing mother snake who was rattling all her rattles. The lizard's tail also heard the rattles. "Why have we come here?" asked the tail. The lizard offered no explanation.

As the rattlesnake fixed her evil stare on the lizard and flicked her tongue in and out in anticipation of a good meal, the lizard was getting ready to throw his tail for the eighty-eighth time.

"You have deceived me!" shouted the tail in a blind rage. "Your promises were all false! Nothing but lies! How can I sacrifice myself for someone who doesn't tell me the truth?"

And so the tail squeezed every one of its muscles just as hard as it could—concentrating desperately to hang on.

At that very moment the lizard attempted to throw his tail. But the tail remained firmly affixed to the lizard's body.

The rattlesnake struck with lightning speed and then swallowed, in a leisurely fashion, the entire lizard.

The Hippopotamus Who Made
Creative Decisions

FULLY SUBMERGED under the surface of an African lake, six bull hippopotamus elders stood on the bottom, their heads close together in the center and their rumps extending out in a circle. The leader, an ancient but still vigorous behemoth, had called this council of hippos to decide on a policy for meeting the threat which an aggressive pride of lions posed to young hippo calves.

The leader enjoyed these decision-making sessions. Feeling the buoyancy of near-weightlessness down in the water, his mind always reached for the most creative solutions. That was why he made the highest level decisions on the bottom of the lake. He called first for a briefing.

"As you know," said a senior hippo advisor, "We have a long-standing dispute with the lions. They charge that we are trampling over their territory and making a muddy mess of it. We say that they shouldn't take any of our hippo calves for their meals."

"What do you recommend?" asked the leader.

"The problem could be resolved by negotiation. We could agree to graze only on the side of the lake which is not lion territory and they would agree to feed only on gazelles, warthogs and zebras."

The meeting was interrupted as the leader permitted his heavy body to float to the surface so that he could take a gulp of air. The other council members readily followed his example. Being less bulky than the leader and having smaller lungs, they needed more frequent breaks for oxygen. But protocol demanded that they go to the surface only when the leader did. Consequently, most council members often felt somewhat giddy in these meetings with their supreme leader.

"What is your view?" the leader inquired of another bull after the meeting resumed at the bottom of the lake.

"I do not believe we should negotiate with the lions. We greatly outweigh them. The preponderance of power is, therefore, clearly with us. It would be a sign of weakness for us to offer to negotiate."

"There is much to what you say," responded the leader. "But it costs nothing to come out for negotiations. In fact, we can demonstrate our good faith that way—and avoid a lot of silly criticism."

"But won't that put us on a muddy slope?" asked one of the hippos. "Couldn't we find ourselves slipping toward agreement?"

"Trust me," said the hippo leader. "I'll do it this way. This evening I will announce a new policy. Naturally I will emphasize that there can be no excuse for the outrageous lion behavior. And there is no chance—in fact, it is unthinkable—that we would reward them by agreeing to sit down with them for negotiations."

The faces of some of the hippo council members were beginning to turn blue from lack of oxygen. The hippo leader nevertheless went on. "And then I will announce the most important part of our policy. I will declare that we will always be ready to negotiate once the lions demonstrate that they intend to conduct themselves like other peaceloving animals. There is no reason that they should not behave like antelopes. That's all they have to do. Nothing more."

The other hippos had their great jaws clamped very tight and their eyes were bulging. Some were afraid they might burst. "And so," concluded the hippo leader, "the choice will be completely up to the lions. Yes, completely up to them."

The leader floated to the surface, and the other council members, following him, gulped greedily for air. It had been an exceptionally long spell on the bottom.

After they descended again, a new member of the council, who was still quite woozy in the head, exclaimed, "What a brilliant strategy! If the lions refuse our offer, it will prove that they are at fault—that they aren't willing to behave like peaceloving animals. But if they are willing to act like antelopes, we'll have gotten everything we want, won't we? Even before the negotiations!"

The hippo leader was pleased with his meeting. Once again, he and his council, experiencing the exhilaration of buoyancy at the bottom of the lake, had come up with a creative solution. The leader always felt that he could accomplish anything in these sessions—as his feet touched lightly on the bottom of the lake.

That night the leader announced his new policy to the rest of the hippo herd and to the pride of lions arrayed by the side of the lake.

The lions, however, could not make any sense out of it. They were also somewhat offended. "Who gave the hippo the right to decide that we have to behave like antelopes?" growled one of the lions. "Yeah," said another, "we're not asking that the hippos behave like gazelles—just that we make a deal."

The lions then spied two young hippo calves. They pounced on them and dragged them off into the bush.

The Giraffe Who Dispensed Advice From High Up

ON THE PLAINS of Africa there lived a giraffe who loved to give advice. He was of an exceptionally lofty stature. Constantly he gazed down at the frailties, follies, and general inadequacies of his fellow creatures.

The other animals, for their part, knew that the giraffe was a formidable creature. They had all seen him dispatch a lion with a single mighty kick. Besides, given his ability to view events from a distance, he clearly was possessed of greater objectivity than others. The advice of such a creature had to be of immeasurable value.

One day the giraffe watched a hungry lion rush at a herd of impala. As was customary with these antelopes when attacked, they began leaping in all directions. They vaulted high above one another and under each other and over bushes and every which way. There was tremendous confusion. The lion, bewildered, lost his prey and slunk away to find an easier victim.

The giraffe then approached the leader of the impala herd and offered the following advice:

"My friend, that was an appalling spectacle. You conveyed no precise message to the lion. Your actions were chaotic. You should have a policy that is clear and coherent. If you communicate such a policy convincingly to the lion, he will then know what actions you will tolerate and which ones you will not."

The impalas pondered this sage advice from their highly respected neighbor. Soon thereafter when a lion approached the herd, an impala stepped forward and, with his front hoof, drew a line in the dirt. He announced to the lion:

"We have adopted a firm policy. We do not wish to be attacked by lions. To make our intentions perfectly clear and so that there may be no misunderstanding, I have drawn a line in the dirt. You must not cross that line!"

The lion, who had been in a crouch, broke into a charge. He rushed across the line, knocked over the impala, and ate him.

The giraffe did not witness this event. He was faraway—advising tortoises how they should deal with their tormentors, the rats. They should not deign to fight with them. They should simply leap away.

The Orangutan Who Believed In Simple Solutions

AN ANCIENT ORANGUTAN who enjoyed great renown as a distinguished jurist often pondered the nature of animal life in the jungle. What he saw as he peered down from his nest in one of the tallest fruit trees deeply disturbed him. Snakes eating birds. Tigers chewing up pigs. Beetles poisoning grasshoppers. Eagles snatching monkeys. Crocodiles crunching turtles. Shrews gobbling up mice.

"There must be a way to put an end to all this chaos and injustice," the orangutan jurist said to himself. "We need a law that will bring happiness to everyone."

And so the orangutan convened a committee of apes, all eminent jurists, to assist him. "What's needed," he told his colleagues, "is a simple concept. It should be a single straightforward rule. If we create a lot of complex provisions, everyone will argue over them and no one will be happy—except the lawyers."

After a lengthy deliberation the committee came up with the following doctrine: "Animals may only eat smaller animals." The idea was that everyone would be most likely to comply with a regulation which permitted doing what was easiest.

The orangutan jurist was pleased with his work. "We have conceived," he declared, "a simple solution. Everyone will be able to understand it." All the other jurists joined in offering their praise. "It's not only simple," said one "it's positively eloquent."

After the new doctrine was promulgated, the crocodiles and the anteaters were, not surprisingly, among its strongest proponents. But some of the small cats complained that they didn't want to give up eating jungle pigs. The mongooses, who killed large

snakes, also protested. But the warrior ants were the most ve-
hement in their denunciation. They devoured everything, big and
small, that didn't get out of their way. As predicted, everyone
understood the new rule, but only the largest animals respected
it. Chaos in the jungle continued.

The old orangutan reconvened his committee of eminent jurists.
"My friends, do not be discouraged. Great new ideas are not always
readily accepted. Perhaps through force of our collective wisdom
we can devise an even better rule."

The committee explored many proposals, but none were satisfactory. Finally, when they were all quite dejected, the orangutan
jurist clutched his brow and, after a profound silence, spoke these
words, "Animals may only eat larger animals." The jurist explained
that there would be much less killing if the regulation permitted
animals to do only what was difficult.

The other jurists were deeply impressed. "This is one of those
inspired ideas," said one of them, "that nobody's ever thought of
before. But once you hear it, you wonder how everyone else could
have missed it."

The warrior ants received the new law with enthusiasm. So also
did the vampire moths who sucked blood from tapirs and large
rodents. But most of the other animals were outraged. The leopards threatened to climb into the jungle canopy and teach the
orangutans a thing or two about realistic rule-making.

For the third time the old orangutan convened his committee
of learned jurists. "There must be a way," he told them, "to find
a simple solution—if only we think hard enough." The committee
conducted a searching review of all animal proclivities. It analyzed,
synthesized, and conceptualized. Brows were deeply furrowed. At
last, after prolonged ratiocination, the orangutan jurist came forth
with the following formulation: "Animals may eat other animals."

The other jurists were beside themselves with praise for their
leader. "It just goes to show," said one, "that if you try hard enough
you can think of anything."

The latest law was applauded by everyone. And so the distinguished orangutan jurist basked in universal praise. Although
chaos continued throughout the jungle, the jurist took no notice
of it. He saw only one thing. All the animals were following his
simple law.

EPILOGUE— DARING TO HOPE

The Dinosaurs Who Had
A Second Chance

ONCE UPON A TIME in the Mesozoic Era, the dinosaurs of the earth got sick of fighting. Some dinosaurs, the ones with larger brains, even feared the extinction of the whole dinosaur race.

And so a plan was hatched by an ultrasaurus, a dinosaur larger than the biggest whale in the ocean. He proposed that the dinosaurs form a parliament where disputes could be resolved through reason and conciliation. All would be equal—the gigantic and the tiny, the ferocious and the timid. A duck-bill dinosaur, when he heard about the plan, questioned whether the earth was ready for such a radical departure from tradition. But he, like all the other dinosaurs, felt he had no choice but to participate in the grand experiment.

At the first session of the dinosaur parliament, the proceedings quickly degenerated into a monumental fracas. Almost immediately the big dinosaurs divided into two opposing camps—the flesh-eaters and the plant-eaters. They forced all the smaller dinosaurs to take sides. When it proved impossible to solve any issue at all, everyone was frustrated. And so in their anger all the dinosaurs began jumping up and down.

Now never on earth had there been an assemblage of so many dinosaurs in one spot. And never had so many ponderous beasts—the ultrasaurs, the supersaurs, the titanosaurs, the diplodocuses, and all the other brontosaurs—jumped up and down in one place.

As the duck-bill dinosaur had feared, the earth was not ready for such an event. Suddenly the earth began to shake and crack. The air was filled with roaring, rasping, tearing sounds which drowned out all the cacophony of the dinosaurs. And then the earth caved in—the first case of significant abuse of the environment by animals.

All the dinosaurs, thousands and thousands of them, fell in. A tremendous whoosh of suction drew them down into a vast black hole. As the dinosaurs tumbled deeper and deeper toward the earth's core, they were observed by God, who had been waiting for them.

God was a small furry mammal. He was Little Bush Baby—a primate with huge round eyes, so he would miss nothing, and a disproportionately large brain, so he could comprehend everything. God unfurled an enormous safety net to catch the descending dinosaurs. His intention was to interview all the fallen creatures and judge which should be saved and which should be pushed through the safety net. Those who weren't saved would drop all the way down to the earth's molten core and be consumed.

God approached the first dinosaur, the huge ultrasaur who had organized the parliament of dinosaurs. "I know that you meant well," said Little Bush Baby, "but before I decide what to do with you I must know something of your deeper feelings, your true aspirations and secret disappointments."

"To tell the truth, God," replied the ultrasaur, "I am fed up with everyone gossiping behind my back about what a tiny brain I have. I know that the earth trembles wherever I tread. But I'd just like others to respect me for once for my mind. I'd like to go back to earth with a big, powerful brain—even if it means I have to have a small, weak body. If you do this for me, I promise that I will use my intellect for everyone's benefit."

Little Bush Baby was impressed by the sincerity of the ultrasaur. And, of course, he had a soft spot for anyone who understood that it was a good thing to have a big brain and who was willing to have a little body. "Okay," he said, "many years from now you will be reincarnated. You will become a new type of creature. You will have the biggest brain that has ever been possessed on earth—and a small, weak body. You will be known as an Atomic Scientist."

Having dealt with one of the biggest of the dinosaurs, God then turned his attention to one of the littlest, a dinosaur no bigger than a chicken.

"And you," asked Little Bush Baby, "if I were to let you live again on earth, what would you like to accomplish?"

"Well," said the miniature dinosaur, "all I do now is run for my life. All the time. Everyone chases me. So I have absolutely no influence on events. I'd like to have more stature. I'd like to make great decisions and see them carried out. I'd like to shape the course of history."

"That's very ambitious," said Little Bush Baby, "but not unworthy. Here's what we'll do. I'll see to it that some time in the future you can become a Great Statesman. You will not have a big body, but you will have a lot of power. You will control things that are called Armies and Navies. Then you will have stature and you will be able to make things happen."

God then turned to a tyrannosaurus rex, an unusually large specimen with a monstrous jaw filled with sharp teeth. "And what have you got to say for yourself?" demanded Little Bush Baby.

"To be perfectly honest," said the tyrannosaur, "I'm sick of being the strongest animal on earth. It creates terrible strains. I just don't want the burdens any longer. I find myself drawn into half the fights up there. Just let me be an ordinary citizen. I want to experience happiness and sorrow, hope and fear, achievement and frustration—just like anyone else."

God was deeply moved by this conversion of the mighty. "Very good," he said. "I have just the slot for you. You will become a creature of limited power—quite limited power. You will become what is known as a Peace Protester."

God had many more cases to deal with. A nodosaur, who was covered with heavy armor plate and who had to crawl close to the ground, was told that he could someday be reincarnated as a Ballerina. A bone-head dinosaur who said he longed to do something more with his skull than bash it against his enemies was promised he could become something called a Psychiatrist. And a megalosaur who said he felt guilty about having disemboweled so many innocent dinosaurs with his claws was given the task of being a Theologian.

One case was particularly difficult for God. In fact, it was the only time he came close to letting a dinosaur fall all the way through to the earth's molten core.

"And you," said Little Bush Baby, "what do you regret about your life on earth? What would you do differently if I gave you another chance?"

God was speaking to a triceratops from whose head stuck out three sharp horns curving upwards in the nastiest way possible. "In fact," answered the triceratops, "I wouldn't do anything differently. To be perfectly frank, God, I really enjoyed sticking it to my enemies."

God was more than a little upset. "But you did terrible damage. Don't you have any regrets about inflicting all those hideous wounds, like the times when you stuck your horns into the bellies of the bone-heads?"

"Not a bit. I enjoyed piercing other dinosaurs ever since I was a child and got my first horns, and then I got better and better at it."

God had heard enough. He was ready to yank the safety net out from under the triceratops. But then he got an idea. "You have one redeeming feature," said Little Bush Baby. "You seem to be honest. Now I know a role for a creature who never shrinks from telling the truth. What would you say to piercing the brains of others? I could make you into a literary figure—a Satirist."

"Well, I don't know," answered the triceratops, who had no idea what God was talking about. "But since you say I can keep on skewering others, I will do my best."

Over time, God interviewed every one of the thousands of dinosaurs who had fallen into the big hole in the earth. And he made assignments for each of them. God was nearly worn out. He wondered if this colossal exertion had been worth the trouble. Yes, all of his dinosaur creatures would have a new opportunity. But what would they make of it?

Many millions of years later, the Atomic Scientists did what came naturally to them. Having once in an earlier incarnation possessed the size of brontosaurs, they instinctively thought big. They used their unprecedented brain power to create bombs that could do even more damage than thousands of brontosaurs jumping up and down in one place.

Now these bombs were possessed by a few of the largest Nations, and the actions of the Nations were under the control of the Great Statesmen. These exalted figures did not, of course, remember that once long ago they had been chicken-size dinosaurs. Still, like the Atomic Scientists, they did what came naturally. They thought small.

Each of the Great Statesmen labored constantly to achieve advantage—no matter how tiny—over his opponents. If his adversary suffered a loss, or appeared to, then the Great Statesman was uplifted. If the Great Statesman's own nation suffered a setback—no matter how minor—that was cause for the deepest alarm. It was about as frightening as being a chicken-size dinosaur chased by a tyrannosaur.

The Great Statesmen pressed the Atomic Scientists to give them the very best bombs, ones that could obliterate the enemy. And they acquired as many of them as they could. Eventually the earth was awash with bombs.

Naturally the Atomic Scientists were proud that they had been able to make explosions that were as brilliant as those that erupted on the face of the sun. But many of them were deeply concerned about what would happen if the bombs ever went off. They did not remember that long ago they had promised God to use their unusually powerful brains for eveyone's benefit. Since that promise was in their bones, so to speak, it created what has come to be called a Conscience.

And so some of the Atomic Scientists organized demonstrations to protest against the building of more and more bombs. They were joined by the other thinking humans, like the Psychiatrists, who had once been bone-head dinosaurs. Great artists also protested, including a Ballerina, who had once been a nodosaur. She was vaguely conscious that it had taken millions of years for creatures like herself to rise up from their bellies and to dance on their toes. She hated the thought that such progress could be wiped away in minutes by the Great Statesmen and their bombs. The Theologians, who had once been ferocious megalosaurs, were prominent in the protests. And, of course, their ranks were swelled by the Peace Protesters, who had once been tyrannosaurs and who were therefore remarkably persistent.

But all of this well-meaning activity accomplished little. It only stimulated the Great Statesmen to sound more sincere in explaining how much they regretted having to build more bombs to protect everyone and how eager they were to get rid of their bombs if only the enemy would do so also.

Not even the Satirists, who had once been triceratops, were able to accomplish anything with their piercing ridicule. Although many citizens thought the criticism of the Satirists was devastating, it did not even scratch the hides of the Great Statesmen. For the Satirists it was humiliating—the Great Statesmen simply ignored them.

Inevitably one day a great crisis occurred between the two largest Nations. It was caused by the desire of each of them to dominate a small Nation which was, as they said, Strategically Situated. The conflict soon became a test of wills. Each of the Great Statesmen feared that he would be ousted from office and reviled by history if it appeared he had behaved like a chicken-size dinosaur. And so each of them ordered that their bombs be readied for use. Of course, they did not want to use them, for that would kill everyone—including themselves. But they felt it was vital that no one think for a moment that they were afraid to.

Now concern about the behavior of the Great Statesmen was not limited to the Atomic Scientists, the Theologians, the Psychiatrists, the Artists, and the Peace Protesters. God himself, Little Bush Baby, was quite alarmed. With his big eyes and brain he had seen and comprehended everything. He knew that if the Great Statesmen slipped up, all of God's creatures could be destroyed. Even God himself might be extinguished. This was not the way things were supposed to go. God was losing control. He had better get a grip on things.

But how? The situation was moving very fast. At any moment one of the Great Statesmen might get rattled and push what had come to be known as the Button, and then God, who would be vaporized along with everyone else, would be helpless. But God was nothing if not resourceful.

It so happened that at the very moment that God was feverishly casting about for an initiative the Great Statesmen were meeting in special enclosures, called War Rooms, together with their senior advisers, many of whom were already fledgling Great Statesmen, and they were debating whether to issue another ultimatum, to launch what in strategic parlance was called a Demonstration Strike, or even whether to fire off all their bombs. In one of the War Rooms a Great Statesman was making a point with some vehemence. In fact, he was pounding the table over and over again with great vigor.

Now, ordinarily, pounding a table, even with tremendous force, would not have much impact beyond the immediate surroundings. But when God became aware of this pounding—and he perceived it instantly—he knew that this was his opening. As the Great Statesman continued to pound the table for emphasis, the War Room began to shake, the floor trembled, and then there was a crescendo of roaring, tearing sounds. The earth cracked open and all the Great Statesmen tumbled in. They fell down and down.

Nearly half way round the globe in the meeting that was simultaneously taking place in the War Room of the other great Nation the discussions had reached a fever pitch. The Great Statesman in charge was angry that his advisers had not prepared for him sufficiently forceful courses of action—what they called Options. And so, in disgust, he picked up the massive bound volume, which was known as the Briefing Book, and with great energy slammed it down on the table.

Once again God was ready. And so the table rocked, the walls of the War Room began to sway, and suddenly a gigantic hole cracked open in the floor. The Great Statesman and all his advisers began descending into the earth.

The two groups of plummeting Statesmen converged about half way down towards the earth's core. God was waiting for them. This was certainly a much easier task than the one God had performed millions of years ago—catching hundreds of thousands of tumbling dinosaurs in a single net.

Little Bush Baby introduced himself to the astonished heap of Great Statesmen:

"I am Bush Baby, God of Earth."

A voice was heard from a corner of the net, "Hah! Hah! That's a good one!"

God was not in the mood to be trifled with. He pulled at the net and the speaker dropped out. His eerie scream as he fell down and down toward the earth's molten core reverberated for some time. In fact, the loss of this particular individual was not an event of much consequence—he was what they called a Vice-President. Nevertheless, Little Bush Baby's decisive action had an arresting impact on the group.

God then laid into his creatures. "What a botch you've made of things! You threaten to destroy not just yourselves, but everything—even me. You probably don't know it, but once before, millions of years ago, you brought on a disaster. You were dinosaurs then. You had a terrible quarrel and lost all control. You were so vociferous and got so frantic, jumping up and down, that you made the crust of the earth crack and cave in. I extended myself. I caught you all with a safety net so you wouldn't melt into nothing at the center of the earth."

God was really wound up. At times Little Bush Baby could be quite loquacious. "And then I transformed you into humans. I was soft. I interviewed you and I acceded to all your requests. Whatever you wanted to be—that's what you'd be. Most of you wanted big brains. So I gave them to you. Big powerful brains. And now what have you done? I ask you—what have you done? You've behaved as if you had no brains at all."

"Yes, we have been inexcusably stupid," interjected a junior Great Statesman who thought a little contrition might help in winning a few points.

"You there," said Little Bush Baby, "pipe down. Nobody asked you to say anything." God did not take kindly to being interrupted.

"And how can you justify building so many bombs to protect yourselves that if they went off you would destroy yourself? You would be safer if you were imbeciles. And for what are you now threatening to end this precious life which I've given you? If you don't get your way completely in running some small Nation that doesn't want either of you, you're going to blow up yourselves, them, and everyone else. This is so crazy that . . . that . . . ," Little Bush Baby began to splutter, "that I just can't believe this is happening."

Now nobody had ever dressed down these Great Statesmen in such scathing terms. They were shocked. And not a little scared. For there they were, down deep in the earth, in a dark hole, suspended in a huge net. Nothing had ever prepared them for this. None of the Great Statesmen could find a single word to utter.

God, who knew everything, could tell what the Great Statesmen were thinking. "You are asking yourselves," said Little Bush Baby, "is he ever going to let us out of here? Are we ever going to see the blue sky again, gaze at the trees in the wind, feel the sun on our faces, caress our loved ones?"

Once again the Great Statesmen could think of nothing to say.

This was fortunate for them—for Little Bush Baby was in no mood to hear petty excuses. If any of the Great Statesmen had given him any lip, undoubtedly he would have let the whole lot of them fall all the way down to the molten core.

"Well, I don't know," said God. "I'm torn. On the one hand, I have my pride. And I'm stubborn. I put a tremendous effort into saving you when you were dinosaurs. You think it was fun going through those thousands and thousands of interviews? Let me tell you, some of it was plain tedious. Many of you were just boring. But I'm a little like everyone else. When I've made a really big effort, I hate to admit I made a mistake.

"On the other hand, " continued Little Bush Baby, "I'm really scared about letting you back up there. You've become a real menace. If I let you fall to your doom right now, you couldn't do any more damage and I'd be through with you. Then I could give my full attention to working with the dolphins, the pigeons, the crickets, and the koala bears, who've never done anything as stupid as you have. That's what would make sense."

Everyone in that dark hole in the earth held their breath. Nothing could be heard save the faint sounds of bubbling, spitting and hissing from the cauldron far below.

"Okay," said Little Bush Baby. "I'm going to let you go back up. You must never, never forget that once you were all dinosaurs together. Now you are all humans together. You will all survive together—or sink together. I hope you appreciate how rare it is in life to get not only a second chance—but a third chance. You can be certain that there will be no fourth chance. Never again will I let you threaten to destroy all the wonderful creatures on earth because you feel you must control some piece of land which you determine to be, as you say, Strategically Situated."

After the Great Statesmen got back to the surface of the earth, things gradually began to change. There were still disputes and occasional wars among the smaller Nations. But when controversies arose between the large nations, which of course they continued to do, the Great Statesmen were possessed of a new impulse to compromise. In their minds a number of images were indelibly fixed. The black hole in the earth—the net which held them suspended above the molten core—the Vice-President's precipitous descent—Little Bush Baby's merciless scolding. The Great Statesmen of both large Nations shared in the knowledge that there was something far worse than running the risk of seeking accomodation with an adversary.

The Great Statesmen thus found the courage to seek common ground with their rivals. Some even summoned the vision to plan together for a better future rather than to nurture grievances of the past. As the Nations of the world, the big ones and the little ones, spent more and more of their time working to solve common problems, the bombs began to rust. The stockpiles began to shrink.

At last, the Great Statesmen were no longer haunted by their past—their ancient humiliations as chicken-size dinosaurs. They created an era of renowned leaders who earned the esteem and gratitude of their peoples. Even Little Bush Baby was pleased. Only one group was disgruntled—the Satirists, who had far fewer follies to write about.